WATCHING THE DEVIL DANCE

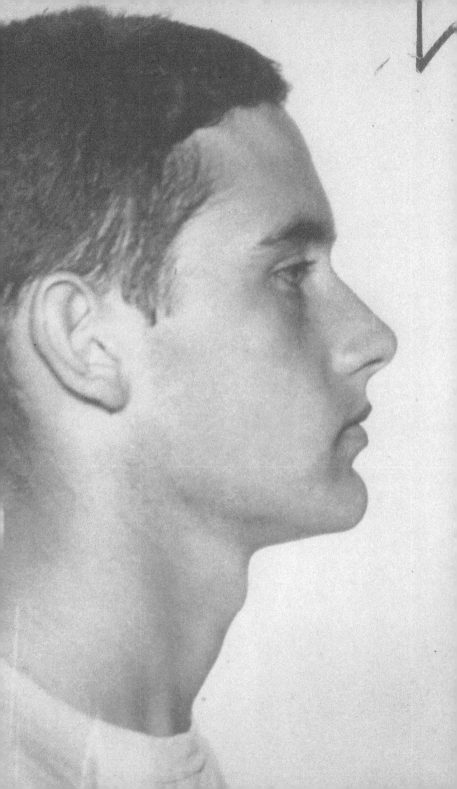

Watching the Devil Dance

How a Spree Killer Slipped Through the Cracks of the Criminal Justice System

Will Toffan

Biblioasis
Windsor, Ontario

FIRST EDITION

Library and Archives Canada Cataloguing in Publication

Title: Watching the devil dance : how a spree killer slipped through the cracks of the criminal justice system / Will Toffan.

Names: Toffan, Will, author.

Description: Includes bibliographical references.

Identifiers: Canadiana (print) 2020028603X | Canadiana (ebook) 20200286102 | ISBN 9781771963251 (softcover) | ISBN 9781771963268 (ebook)

Subjects: LCSH: Lamb, Matthew Charles, 1948-1976. | LCSH: Mass murder—Ontario—Windsor—History—20th century. | LCSH: Mass shootings—Ontario—Windsor—History—20th century. | LCSH: Spree murderers—Ontario—Windsor—Biography. | LCSH: Criminal justice, Administration of—Ontario—History—20th century.

Classification: LCC HV6535.C33 W54 2020 | DDC 364.152/340971332—dc23

Edited by Sharon Hanna
Copyedited by Chandra Wohleber
Cover and text designed by Michel Vrana
Cover and frontispiece image (Matthew Charles Lamb's 1966 mugshot) used courtesy of the *Windsor Star*.

Published with the generous assistance of the Canada Council for the Arts, which last year invested $153 million to bring the arts to Canadians throughout the country, and the financial support of the Government of Canada. Biblioasis also acknowledges the support of the Ontario Arts Council (OAC), an agency of the Government of Ontario, which last year funded 1,709 individual artists and 1,078 organizations in 204 communities across Ontario, for a total of $52.1 million, and the contribution of the Government of Ontario through the Ontario Book Publishing Tax Credit

PRINTED AND BOUND IN CANADA

CONTENTS

PREFACE

IN 1974, I WAS A NINETEEN-YEAR-OLD LAD, a rookie officer of the Royal Canadian Mounted Police. I was assigned to patrol the small logging towns carved by nature and man throughout northern British Columbia, when I found myself at the epicenter of what was—and today remains—the most active region for serial killers in Canada. The northern city of Prince George is the starting point for Highway 16, a sinister stretch of road connecting central BC to the port city of Prince Rupert on the Pacific coast—a distance of approximately 700 kilometres. Today, this lonely stretch is known as the infamous "Highway of Tears," where at least eighteen young women have been designated as victims of serial killers, dating back to 1969. Unofficially, more than fifty women—many of them from nearby reservations—have been considered probable victims of serial homicide by predators hunting on Highway 16. This is where I began my career in law enforcement, but it was not my first brush with murder and a cold-blooded killer.

Let's go back to the summer of 1966 in my hometown of Windsor, Ontario. The city sits on the southern shore of the Detroit River, straddling the international border between Canada and the United States. From Windsor's waterfront, one can peer across the Detroit River, barely one kilometre wide, and watch the cars driving down the streets of Detroit's once vibrant commercial district. In 1966, Windsor was home to just under two hundred thousand people, slightly less than its current population. In the 1960s and 1970s, it was Canada's automotive capital, producing General Motors, Ford Motor Company, and Chrysler vehicles supported by a world-class tool-and-die industry. With an unemployment rate below 5 percent, Windsor was an industrial powerhouse offering well-paid employment, job security, and a middle-class lifestyle seemingly to anyone with a pulse and a willingness to get out of bed in the morning.

Supported by a thriving industrial sector, Windsor's commercial district was in the midst of a construction boom in the summer of 1966. I distinctly recall receiving my first real camera, a 35mm Kodak, for my eleventh birthday. I caught the bus downtown and climbed to the top floor of a new parking garage across the street from Steinberg's department store. I snapped numerous photographs of Windsor's rapidly changing skyline and hung the pictures on my bedroom wall. I was very proud of my city. My civic pride and enthusiasm were certainly shared, as every municipal election at the time produced at least one candidate promising to rectify the disparity between Detroit's towering skyscrapers and Windsor's comparatively unimpressive cityscape. Unfortunately, Windsor's zeal for commercial growth and inferiority complex vis-à-vis Detroit resulted in the destruction of beautiful historic brownstones and regal hotels, leaving our city's skyline scarred. And yet there was no denying Windsor was a city on the move. Seen in retrospect, the 1960s were Windsor's golden age.

Windsor was certainly the car capital of Canada, but in 1966, Detroit, Michigan, was the automotive capital of the world. The Motor City boasted a population of 1.8 million, with Detroit car manufacturers claiming a 90 percent global market share. Their factories pumped out thirteen million vehicles annually. Every weekend, Windsorites would cross the border to shop in the always crowded retail stores of downtown Detroit. Sidewalks were crammed with people as street vendors along Woodward Avenue sold bags of hot peanuts and chestnuts roasted on the spot in mobile pushcart ovens. Detroit's movie theatres—a favourite destination for pubescent boys from Windsor—did a brisk business offering titillating "sexploitation" films unavailable in Canada. Detroit was also the birthplace of a pop music genre that would gain a global following in the 1960s. The "Motown sound" and its multiple platinum record productions were written and recorded in a small, unimpressive residence located on West Grand Boulevard in the northwest section of downtown Detroit. Local Black artists such as Stevie Wonder, Smokey Robinson, Diana Ross and the Supremes, and the Temptations skyrocketed to international fame. Tragically, the optimism and verve that defined Detroit in the mid-1960s would all come crashing down with the riots of summer 1967, marking the beginning of Detroit's slow, inexorable decline. The increase in property destruction and violent crime, its stigma as America's homicide capital, the "White flight" to the suburbs, and Detroit's crumbling infrastructure were symptomatic of the city's systemic political corruption and diminishing tax revenues. But that was all in the future. No one could have foreseen the fate awaiting Detroit or Windsor as the warm spring days of 1966 slipped into June, when Matthew Charles Lamb loaded his uncle's shotgun and set out on a shooting spree on the residential streets of Windsor. There are many reasons why this true crime story deserves historical review, yet my initial motive for revisiting this crime was of a personal nature. The first victim to die at the hands of Matthew Charles Lamb was my next-door neighbour and first adolescent crush.

I first met the Chaykoski family in 1965 when they moved into the upper apartment of the duplex next door to my family home at 1044 Gladstone Avenue, located in a working-class neighbourhood where families kept the grass cut and cleared their sidewalks of snow from the rare storms that periodically marred Windsor's traditionally mild winters. I quickly became good friends with the youngest of the family, Richard Chaykoski. Richard shared the apartment with his older sister Edith and their mother, also named Edith. Three elder siblings had already moved on with their own lives. I never met the father and it soon became evident the Chaykoskis were a single-parent family. Admittedly, my most vivid memory of my friendship with Richard had little to do with him. It was the day he introduced me to his nineteen-year-old sister Edith. She was seated on the couch in the living room of their apartment with one or two other girls. Edith was wearing a blue uniform with matching blouse and an impressive hat. I thought she was a nurse. When introduced, she turned and smiled at me and said hello before returning to converse with her friends. I was smitten. I was eleven years old, pushing twelve, and funny feelings in my physiology had begun to stir. Watching Edith from my bedroom window across the street, I would often see her standing at the bus stop. She possessed all the attributes quickly becoming a main focus of my developing interest in girls.

My one intimate moment with Edith Chaykoski was sometime in the summer of 1965. Edith was walking up the alley toward the corner bus stop. Presumably, she was on her way to work at the nursing home, wearing that eye-catching blue uniform. I was riding my new Mustang bicycle with the revolutionary leopard-skin banana seat, with a Davy Crockett coonskin tail dangling from the rear passenger hand bar, which swung back and forth from air gusts generated when pedalling the bike at top speed. I always wore a plastic Ratfink ring on the middle finger of my left hand, prominently displayed and menacing when wrapped around the bicycle handgrip. I raced down the alley at full speed to catch up to Edith, with my six-dollar transistor radio taped to the handlebars cranked at full volume to CKLW-AM blasting "The Morning Sun Is Shining Like a Red Rubber Ball," by The Cyrkle. This was my chance! I was at the top of my game and loaded for bear. I raced up alongside Edith and hit my brakes, kicking up a cloud of dust, startling her. Confident I had impressed her with my devil-may-care attitude, I offered her a ride on my bike for the final four metres to the bus stop. She let me down gently, politely explaining she couldn't chance wrinkling or getting bicycle grease on her uniform; a convincing rationale. The Chaykoskis moved away shortly thereafter. That was the last time I saw Edith Chaykoski alive.

The killing spree that occurred in Windsor in June 1966 received widespread media attention at the time, yet has been largely forgotten save for those directly affected by the crime itself. The controversial post-offence legacy of the killer briefly attracted international media attention again in 1976, a decade after the shooting spree occurred. Pertinent facts of this once highly publicized "spree killer" case, withheld from the public, are documented here for the first time. These pages will reveal the human folly within a legal system struggling to understand a new kind of killer responsible for a crime virtually unheard of in 1966. This era of radical social change was also what made the crime's barely conceivable aftermath possible. Matthew Charles Lamb was Canada's first, and most controversial, spree killer. The Lamb killings were Cassandra warnings; portents of things to come. Lamb's 1966 murder rampage was the first example of what would become a paradigm shift across North America, as a new "type" of homicide and killer captured the popular imagination—and continues to plague the streets.

The spree killings of 1966 remain seared in the collective memory of those of us old enough to have lived through them. People interviewed who were young adults at the time of these murders mostly recall pleasing memories of carefree days, first loves, and juvenile escapades fueled by alcohol or hallucinogenic drugs—the latter fast becoming the consciousness-altering choice of the 1960s counterculture. Memories of 1966 are forever linked with favourite songs during this era of musical creativity, yet tempered by an evocative sadness. When the Lamb spree killings are discussed, every person I spoke with clearly recalled where they were and what they were doing when this bizarre crime occurred.

My tape recorder in hand, I conducted many interviews with people directly involved with the Lamb case to uncover the real story of what happened that fateful night. Many of these people were retired law enforcement—the likes of Windsor Police Superintendent Jim Ure, Detective Sergeant Ken Farrow, Detective Frank Chauvin, Detective Al Proctor, and Chief of Police Jack Shuttleworth—who all provided insights into the Lamb case unobtainable from secondary source materials. Justice Saul Nosanchuk, defence counsel for Lamb, gave numerous interviews, sharing his personal notes and opinions. I was even able to speak with a survivor and with one of Lamb's childhood friends. With my history in law enforcement, it was like working a case again, interviewing the primary sources to piece together the truth. Many of my interview subjects have since passed on, but their memories of Lamb's crimes and the aftermath live on in the pages of this book.

For Windsor police investigators with firsthand knowledge of this case, men now well into their eighties and nineties, their reality during the 1960s was very different. Police officers live in an unpredictable and often vicious world where one deals only with the worst of people or people at their worst. Police officers know the two inevitable rules that parents instinctively deny. Rule number one is: Really bad things can happen to innocent children. Rule number two is: Parents and police cannot change rule number one. These now retired officers discussed the Lamb case particulars with modulated voices and a professional air of detachment common to all police officers—an essential coping mechanism for performing one's job effectively. However, whenever these investigators recalled a particular aspect of the Lamb killings that still riled, or that triggered memories from a totally unrelated crime, an emotional purge would follow, revealing their inability to reconcile and put to rest a very personal, spiritually unresolved issue that still haunts them. Every veteran police officer carries this burden, and it is a testament to their humanity. I call it the "Lawman's Ghost."

I have ghosts of my own. When I was posted in March 1975 to Terrace, BC, one of many towns situated along the Highway of Tears, one of the earliest victims of these sexual/serial killers, reported missing in December 1974, was a young local girl named Monica Ignas. In April 1975, her remains were found. She had been strangled with her own clothing. The Terrace RCMP detachment was a thirty-man force, with three officers in the General Investigative Unit (GIS) assigned to investigative this homicide. I often accompanied the homicide officers working this case file, interviewing potential suspects and following any leads, no matter how thin. Local small-time criminals were the focus of the investigation, yet given the lack of physical evidence at the scene, all inquiries led nowhere. Both the police and citizens were as yet unaware of the scope of the evil plaguing this region, and ill-equipped to deal with it given the limited investigative and forensic tools then available to police. While a killer responsible for other murders along this forsaken stretch was discovered in 2012, and may be the guilty party here as well, Monica Ignas's murder remains a cold case that my fellow officers have never been able to solve.

Part of my job was to give lectures to young women in high schools around Prince Rupert, explaining what the police understood about rapists and the steps women could take to avoid becoming victims—even though we remained unaware of how dangerous the region had become. At the time, although terminology such as *serial rapist, serial killer,* or *spree killer* was not yet in widespread use, or even understood, by 1976, the RCMP had nevertheless developed its own rudimentary classification system for various types of rapists and the disordered personalities that commit these crimes. Even then, we recognized the psychology of the offender as key to understanding the problem. Our work formed the basis of the classifications the RCMP use today. Even back in 1976, some ten years after Matthew Charles Lamb rocked my childhood, setting me on the path toward law enforcement, I was working to understand the minds of murderers, rapists, and criminal psychopaths. With this book, I am going back to that first ghost that haunted me, to tell the whole story for the first time—now informed by modern understandings of criminal psychology.

The shooting spree by Matthew Lamb on the evening of June 25, 1966, was a crime as rare as it was cruel, followed by a bizarre ten-year odyssey one *Globe and Mail* reporter would aptly cite as "a story too unbelievable to be fiction." For those of us who do remember, these young victims were from our time and our city. They were our children, our friends, our neighbours, robbed of life in a crime that took away everything they had or ever would have, leaving only a trail of damaged and still grieving family members, friends, and police officers as their collective epitaph. This is their story.

CHAPTER ONE:
Prelude to Disaster

WITH ONLY HOURS LEFT TO LIVE, TWENTY-YEAR-old Edith Chaykoski had a premonition of her imminent fate. Seated at her vanity table in the townhouse she shared with her mother and younger brother, Edith suddenly cried out, "I can't see myself! Mom, I can't see myself!" Edith's mother, startled by the panic in her daughter's voice, rushed into the room. With her finger, Edith repeatedly stabbed at her mirror. "I was doing my makeup," she sobbed, "and I disappeared in the mirror. There's no reflection! I wasn't there!" Edith sought comfort in her mother's assurances that she was somehow mistaken. Still shaken and unconvinced, Edith stated she didn't feel like going out that Saturday evening after all, even though she had been looking forward to visiting her elder brother Kenneth and his wife, Charmaine, then eight months pregnant with their first child. Mrs Chaykoski insisted her daughter go out and socialize, as Edith had worked long hours that week at the nursing home where she was employed as a nurses' aide.

For the rest of her life, Mrs Chaykoski would retell this story to family and friends, as if seeking redemption for having persuaded Edith to visit her brother that Saturday night. She took little solace in their promises that they would have given the same advice to their own children. Haunted by the loss of her beloved daughter and namesake, Mrs Chaykoski would begin to lose her long battle with alcohol, seeking temporary release from the constant yearning for the words of forgiveness that could never come.

In the spring of 1966, the Chaykoskis had moved from their upstairs duplex at 1038 Gladstone Avenue into a rented townhouse on Monmouth Road, in a neglected section of the otherwise elegant neighbourhood of Walkerville. A company town built and financed by its founder, whisky baron Hiram Walker, many of the homes still retain their nineteenth-century character—tasteful historical relics of the ostentatious wealth once concentrated there. Two blocks of identical semi-detached brownstone townhouses on Monmouth Road, originally built in 1859 to house Hiram Walker's unskilled labour force, unofficially constituted Walkerville's eastern boundary. By the mid-twentieth century, these townhouses had fallen into a state of disrepair, rented to tenants on low or fixed incomes by absentee landlords. It was here that Mrs Chaykoski, her daughter Edith, and youngest son, Richard, took up new residence.

Throughout the 1950s, Mr and Mrs John and Edith Chaykoski had raised Edith and her four siblings on Ford Boulevard in east Windsor. Mr Chaykoski owned an appliance repair shop on the same street, earning just enough to provide for his family. By the early 1960s, though, marital problems and financial pressures forced the family's breakup. Two of Edith's older siblings—a married sister and the eldest brother, who was serving with the Canadian Armed Forces—had already moved on with their own lives, leaving just Edith and the youngest brother, Richard, in their mother's care. Edith's other older brother, Kenneth, and his new spouse, Charmaine, remained on Ford Boulevard, intent on raising their soon-to-be-born child in the familiar sights and smells evoking happier days in the Chaykoski family's old neighbourhood.

Edith Chaykoski left her home at 744 Monmouth Road for the last time in the early evening hours of June 25, 1966. With an unenthusiastic wave goodbye to her mother, she hurried to catch the bus to her brother's home at 1635 Ford Boulevard. The oppressive humidity of a typical Windsor summer evening hung heavy in the air, sticky and sluggish. It was too hot to socialize indoors as home air conditioners were virtually non-existent, and the heavy iron fans then available were both expensive and dangerous, especially to the fingers of curious children. The Chaykoskis talked in their backyard until 10 p.m. when Edith announced she was leaving and would walk the five blocks south to Tecumseh Road to catch the bus home. Setting out alone, she began walking past familiar sturdy working-class homes with sizable front porches where residents typically exchanged greetings and gossip.

As an afterthought, Ken and Charmaine Chaykoski decided to accompany Edith to the bus stop and, having caught up, the three crossed the street, where they met neighbours Vincent Franco, Don Mulesa, and Andrew Woloch. The three young men were standing outside Woloch's home, debating whether to walk to the A&W drive-in on Tecumseh Road, a popular weekend hangout where young men in straight-legged cuffed blue jeans and ducktail haircuts flaunted their customized cars, or to go for a drink at the nearby Canada Tavern, which boasted a "colour" television set where patrons could watch live telecasts of *Hockey Night in Canada*.

Twenty-one-year-old Andrew "Andy" Woloch was modest and well-liked, the acknowledged leader of the group, and a second-year honour student already studying for the upcoming 1966 autumn semester at the University of Windsor's Faculty of Engineering. A well-known Windsor athlete with a keen intellect, Woloch had been a star player in the Windsor softball

3

leagues and a top forward on the Junior "B" Hockey circuit. As an undergraduate, he was named outstanding player and top scorer on the University of Windsor hockey team for both the 1965 and 1966 seasons.

Don Mulesa, also twenty-one years of age, was completing a business degree from the Ontario Institute of Technology, known today as St. Clair College. As a child, he had lost one eye to illness, but it was not a barrier to his athletic or academic prowess. A bright student, Mulesa was interested in early computer technology. Friends from childhood, Woloch and Mulesa shared a Ukrainian heritage and mutual interest in sports and technical academics. To this day, Mulesa dislikes speaking about the events of June 25, 1966.

Vincent Franco, nineteen years of age, was born in Trinidad and Tobago to parents of Spanish and Portuguese descent. Franco never met his father, who was killed while riding his bicycle by a carload of intoxicated British girls touring the Caribbean islands just two months before Franco was born. In 1954, Franco's mother arrived in Canada with Vincent, then seven years old, and his two older sisters. Mrs Franco purchased a home on Ford Boulevard and would build a successful career as chief bookkeeper for Meretsky's Furniture Retail. A bit younger than his friends, Franco was also academically astute and well-liked.

Like most Canadian boys at the time, the three young men had spent much of their youth honing their hockey skills on frozen rivers or backyard ice rinks. Woloch's talent was immediately apparent to Mulesa and Franco, who struggled to keep up during hockey scrimmages played on iced-over ponds in the open fields between Ford Boulevard and Ferndale Avenue, a then largely undeveloped area collectively owned by a few local Ukrainian families. Woloch's mother maintained a large orchard there, selling the produce to neighbours and local grocers to help pay for Andrew's schooling and the family's bills.

As Franco and Woloch chatted with Ken and Charmaine Chaykoski outside the Woloch home that Saturday night, Don

Mulesa and Edith Chaykoski enjoyed exchanging memories of St. Theresa Elementary school, which they had attended together as children. Still undecided between A&W or the Canada Tavern, the three men decided to join the three Chaykoskis, and together, the six friends walked south toward Tecumseh Road. They would never reach it.

CHAPTER TWO:
Saturday-Night Massacre

EIGHTEEN-YEAR-OLD MATTHEW CHARLES LAMB was in an ugly mood as he left work that Saturday afternoon, walking home in the sweltering heat to 1912 Ford Boulevard. Temporarily residing with his uncle, Lamb had been released early from Kingston federal penitentiary just seventeen days earlier, having served fourteen months of a two-year sentence. Required to obtain employment as a condition of his parole, Lamb had grudgingly accepted a position as an apprentice woodworker. Incensed at being asked to work overtime that Saturday afternoon—having already worked overtime that week—he declined what he considered to be an unreasonable request by his employer. The young ex-convict was also depressed about his job: a skilled trade requiring two years' apprenticeship before certification, followed by what Lamb perceived as years of drudgery working as a skilled craftsman—a future for which he felt nothing but contempt.

Lamb arrived home at approximately 3 p.m., having previously agreed to babysit that evening for his uncle, Stanley Hasketh. He proceeded to down eight bottles of beer over the next six hours, put six-year-old Chucky and three-year-old Amy Hasketh to bed, and watch a violent television western until 9 p.m., before retiring to bed and falling fast asleep. Less than an hour had passed before Lamb abruptly awoke, got out of bed, and removed his uncle's double-barrelled shotgun from the hall closet. He grabbed the ammunition box from the closet's top shelf and emptied the box of shotgun shells onto the kitchen table. Loading both barrels of the shotgun and stuffing his pockets full of ammunition, Lamb left his uncle's residence at approximately 10:15 p.m., and walked out into the night.

One block south was Tecumseh Road, one of Windsor's busiest thoroughfares and a favourite spot for teenagers congregating outside local taverns or the popular Hi Ho Diner. Had he walked a block south toward the bright lights of Tecumseh Road, Lamb would have confronted numerous potential victims and the opportunity to expend all the shotgun shells in his bulging pockets in one frenzied act of carnage.

Instead, he began walking north on the east side of Ford Boulevard, crossing Coronation Street, where he was immediately confronted by Michael and Jack Lehoux—ten and six years old respectively. The two brothers were playing in the front yard of their home located at 1884 Ford Boulevard. Their parents, Dennis and Imelda Lehoux, were entertaining four friends in the garden directly adjacent to their home.[1] The boys watched as Lamb crossed Coronation Avenue and walked in their direction. Michael recalled what transpired next:

> I thought he held what appeared to be a stick or club as
> he approached. Jack recognized Lamb first as he was

---

1   In the mid-1970s, Dennis Lehoux built the brick home currently on Ford Boulevard, where their garden stood in 1966.

best friends with Chucky Hasketh, the six-year-old son of Mr [Stanley] Hasketh. I was older and didn't play with the Hasketh children much. Ford Boulevard is a very dark street at night and I only recognized him when he came right up to us, and only then realized Lamb was holding a rifle—not a club or stick.

Younger brother Jack vaguely realized it was a gun, but being only six years old, he was oblivious to the real danger of what that meant and the dangerous situation in which the brothers now found themselves. Jack recalls what happened next:

I recognized the man as Chucky's uncle [...] I used to go over to their home all the time to play with Chucky. That's where I was introduced to Lamb a couple of weeks earlier. When he came up to us that night, I said, "Hi, Uncle Matt," as that's what Chucky and his little sister called him. He [Lamb] just let out a growl or a snicker— like an animal. He didn't say anything else. He stared at me and I stared back. I wasn't scared and scarcely recognized the object stuck in my face to be a gun.

In this momentary standstill, shotgun fixed on the young boy, Lamb likely would have spotted the three adult couples talking in the garden, only metres away. Did he recognize the childhood friend of his nephew? Jack continues:

I was only six! I was too young to react in any other manner, but that growl scared me. [...] As I remember it, Lamb lowered his gun and walked around me, as I was blocking the sidewalk.

The Lehoux brothers may just have saved the lives of their parents and guests that night, even though Jack now speculates that it was he and his family who may have woken Lamb from his slumber in the first place. "I believe it was my family that woke Lamb up or attracted his attention when he emerged from his house," he surmises. "We made a lot of noise. I also think Lamb never shot me because I was too young to be scared and/or because he knew who I was [...] best friends with his nephew." Whatever the reason, Lamb moved on.

Lamb continued walking a short distance, attracted to the bright lights, voices, and loud music emanating from a nearby outdoor garage, where Mr and Mrs Leo Suchiu of 1864 Ford Boulevard were celebrating their twenty-fifth wedding anniversary with friends and family. The streetlights are located on the opposite side of this residential street, and even with the brighter bulbs in use today, the lights' glare does not extend beyond the centre of the road, leaving the east side of Ford Boulevard perpetually shrouded in darkness. Lamb stopped walking barely fifty metres from where he began, halting just short of the Suchius' brightly lit front yard, his silhouette obscured by the cover of a young tree in front of the neighbouring home at 1872 Ford Boulevard. Stepping slightly back off the sidewalk—his loaded shotgun cradled in his left arm— Lamb then pivoted right, his weapon and full attention now fixed on the numerous celebrants crowded in and around the Suchius' open detached garage. He observed as the revellers, completely unaware of their stalker, merrily conversed and milled in and out of the house via the Suchius' side entrance just a few paces from the garage. Waiting for the opportune moment to attack, Lamb pondered his next move.

Approaching at a quick pace from the opposite direction with his five companions, Vincent Franco recalls how the bright lights from the Suchiu residence illuminated the unusually large number of cars haphazardly parked on both sides of Ford Boulevard, in sharp contrast to the night shadows of the otherwise tranquil surroundings. Stepping briskly out from the darkness, the six pedestrians briefly looked left to view the ongoing festivities in the open-garage party while they continued walking. Their unexpected approach surprised Lamb as a collision between the two parties was now unavoidable. Official media accounts the following day would prematurely—and incorrectly—conclude that Lamb had been hiding in ambush behind the tree in front of 1872 Ford Boulevard, lying in wait for the Chaykoski party to come within gun range before opening fire. The truth is far more terrifying: "I swear on my life until my dying day," Franco declared emphatically, "that we prevented a terrible massacre that night. If it wasn't for us walking out of the dark when we did and surprising Lamb, at least twenty people would have died that night. Of that I am absolutely convinced." He continues, "Lamb was in front of us with a perfect view of the party going on in the garage. They were his target, not us, like the papers led people to believe. Lamb could not have been standing beside that tree waiting for us, as it was impossible to see past the lights from the party from either direction, so if we couldn't see past them, neither could he!"

Lamb's inability to see the group's approach from the north would have been further obstructed by the bright side porch lights from the Suchiu home (since removed), further restricting his field of vision. "He couldn't have seen us coming. We walked out from the dark too fast," Franco indignantly remarks, before his voice suddenly drops to a barely audible whisper; "Then Lamb saw us."

Startled by the unexpected crowd of people bearing down on him, Lamb was forced to improvise. Spinning around to his left, Lamb pointed his shotgun directly at Edith Chaykoski and Don Mulesa, who were walking together at the front of the group, and barked, "Hands up!" Everyone except Edith immediately stopped walking, although no one had time to raise their hands before Lamb fired. Edith Chaykoski likely assumed Lamb was a drunken party guest acting out a tasteless gag or prank, given the jovial atmosphere around the Suchiu residence. Not one to suffer fools, Chaykoski ignored Lamb and tried walking around him—when Lamb fired. The shotgun blast struck Chaykoski directly in the stomach at such close range that the shotgun pellets from the fired cartridge did not have time to disperse, confirmed by the autopsy the following day. In short, she took a "full load" at point-blank range. The force of the blast hurled her forward onto the sidewalk where she lay bleeding on her shredded stomach with only her legs and lower torso illuminated by the Suchius' outdoor lights. Her upper body lay obscured in darkness, concealing her face half-buried in the loose topsoil that nourished the neatly planted row of flowers in front of 1872 Ford Boulevard, the house next door to the Suchiu residence.

For twenty seconds, it seemed that time stood still. No one, including Lamb, uttered a sound or moved a muscle. The noise from the shotgun blast and the sight of Chaykoski's body splayed across the sidewalk overwhelmed the senses in a scene made more macabre by the continuous laughter emanating from the nearby celebrations. Lamb kept his shotgun pointed at the group as each potential victim—crippled by shock—struggled to make sense of their predicament. Charmaine Chaykoski, eight months pregnant, now stood directly in the killer's sights as Edith, who had been walking in front of her, now lay motionless at her feet. She studied the assailant's face, watching for any twitch or move-ment that might betray the killer's next move, desperate for any opportunity to save the life of her unborn child. Standing far-ther back, Franco's eyes were fixed on Lamb's shotgun, which he initially believed to be a popular toy gun sold at the time:

> Remember those really cool toy guns sold back then?
> They looked like shotguns or those old-fashioned
> muskets. They had a piece of cork attached to a long
> string. You shoved the cork into the barrel, and when
> you fired, the cork made a really loud "popping" sound
> as it flew out of the barrel. That's what I thought it was
> when Lamb first fired. Even when I saw Edith fall to the
> ground, I initially thought she was just playing along
> with the joke. I suppose at first none of us wanted to
> accept what was really happening.

The five remaining souls, stunned by the sight of Chaykoski's body lying motionless on the sidewalk, now faced the fight-or-flight option—a life-and-death decision made more difficult as initial shock gave way to paralyzing fear.

Today, Franco remains haunted by the terrified look of Woloch, who was likely the first victim to recognize the gravity of their situation. The fear so evidently etched on his friend's face triggered Franco's survival instincts. Shaking off his stupor, Franco surreptitiously began sidestepping to his right to present a more difficult target should Lamb start firing on the group. Woloch's terrified expression may have saved Franco's life, but it doomed Woloch. Breaking the silence after shooting Edith Chaykoski, Lamb once again shouted, "Hands up!" Panic-stricken, Woloch was the only one of the group to immediately obey, thrusting his arms above his head and in doing so, sealing his fate. This sudden movement caught Lamb's attention. Redirecting his aim and firing, Lamb's second shotgun blast struck Woloch in the abdomen from a distance of two metres. The shotgun shell now had time to disperse, its pellets also striking Kenneth Chaykoski in the right arm and hip.

Lamb would later admit to psychiatrists his most vivid memory of the killing spree was the expression of pure terror frozen on a young man's face, followed by him "somehow" firing directly into the man's abdomen. This was a revealing comment on Lamb's part, exposing the latent sadism that is a key marker of a psychopathic personality. Andrew Woloch's immediate compliance with Lamb's order to raise his hands was the act of a terrified young man who Lamb knew posed no threat, yet nevertheless chose to shoot anyway. It can be argued Edith Chaykoski was shot when she challenged Lamb's control over the situation by ignoring him. Shooting Woloch suggests Lamb—knowingly or not—was gratifying his long-festering violent fantasies of total control over the fate of others. Today, we commonly know this as the "God complex." The power rush of control over a stranger's life or death is a primary motive for all spree killers. And Lamb was just beginning his rampage.

The second shot woke the victims from their paralyzing stupor. Watching Woloch go down, Franco sprinted to the bright lights of the Suchius' porch just as a party guest, a local Hungarian priest, was opening the inside door, intent on returning to the party in the garage. Unaware of the shootings outside, the priest found himself confronted by a frantic Franco, shouting warnings of a shooter and alerts about his wounded friends, demanding that the porch lights be turned off or everyone would be killed. The priest tried to restrain the agitated Franco who, upon breaking free from the priest's grasp, grabbed one of the empty beer bottles lined atop the wooden porch step. Smashing the top off the bottle to use as a crude weapon, Franco ran back to help the gravely wounded Woloch bleeding on the sidewalk. A wounded Ken Chaykoski and Charmaine ran to the garage where the celebrations continued in full swing. Amidst all the noise and revelry, no one at the party had thought to look outside the garage door to investigate the two gunshots; most assumed someone from the party was just setting off firecrackers as a celebratory gesture. When Ken and Charmaine Chaykoski burst into the garage seeking help, some of the guests disapprovingly ignored these "party crashers," annoyed by their hysteria about a "madman killer" lurking just outside the garage door. It was not until someone noticed the blood on Ken's clothing from gunshot wounds that the party gave way to pandemonium. The raucous laughter turned to screams as frightened party guests groped about in the darkness after someone turned off the interior garage lights to prevent the celebrants becoming a target of the unknown shooter. Word quickly spread that a crazed killer was in their midst.

Don Mulesa ran right past Lamb following the second shotgun blast, and dashed onto the porch of 1872 Ford Boulevard, banging on the front door and calling for the occupant to call the police. A woman opened the door a crack, saying there was no telephone in the home, before shutting the door in his face, leaving Mulesa to his fate.

In an unfortunate coincidence, the Windsor Police were operating with a skeleton crew that evening. It was Awards Night, the biggest night of the year on the Windsor Police Department's social calendar, attended by officers of every rank as well as the city's business, political, and cultural elite. Outside, a deafening cacophony of flashing lights and sirens echoed throughout the city as all available police, fire, and ambulance units from Windsor's surrounding districts responded to frantic appeals from Windsor Police radio dispatchers. The vehicles converged on the 1800 block of Ford Boulevard. Lolly Robinet, a high school student in 1966, was earning money babysitting at a Riverside home approximately one kilometre from the unfolding tragedy. "I'll never forget that night," she declares, "and all the different sirens seemingly coming out of nowhere and from every direction. I ran out onto the porch and all I saw were people from neighbouring homes, like me, trying to ascertain where the speeding police cars and ambulances were all going. You instinctively knew something very, very serious had happened."

The first unmarked police vehicle arrived at the crime scene just as Franco was trying to resuscitate Woloch's motionless body. To the eyes of the first police detective, there was a young man, broken bottle in hand, standing over a prostrate body. Sneaking up behind Franco, he grabbed and held the young man in a bear hug, ignoring Franco's insistent pleas that he be released to go after the killer. Once officers were satisfied he was not a suspect, Franco was released from the detective's stranglehold and proceeded to convey, as best he could, what had just transpired. This brave detective had momentarily mistaken Franco for an assailant, based on the optics when police first arrived on scene. Fortunately for Franco, this detective's quick-thinking response, rather than reaching for his weapon, prevented another gunshot tragedy.

When Vincent Franco now speaks about that night, he always prefaces his recollections by emphasizing the strong childhood bond between himself, Don Mulesa, and Andrew Woloch. He speaks of Woloch with a tone of reverence and loss, bragging of his friend's remarkable stick-handling skills and speed on the hockey rink. Franco still questions the merit of his own actions immediately following the deadly confrontation with Lamb, concerned that he had been cowardly, doubting his instinct to get help. Weighed down by survivor's guilt, Franco regrets having left Woloch lying on the sidewalk as he ran to the Suchui home to find aid for his fallen friends. For the past fifty years, until our interview, he had been unaware of a media account extolling his heroic actions that night, lauding his courage at age nineteen for returning, ready to help and defend his wounded friends, while the gunman was believed to be still lurking in the immediate area.

For his part, Don Mulesa cautiously emerged from the rear of 1872 Ford Boulevard and ran over to Chaykoski's body. Raising her half-buried face from the flowers bordering the sidewalk, Mulesa turned Edith over onto her back. She tried to speak, but could only mumble a few unintelligible words before fading back into unconsciousness. Mrs Dupuis of 1872 Ford Boulevard now emerged from her home and went over to the prostrate body of Chaykoski. Jack Lehoux, having run down to the street with his father and brother after the chaos erupted, witnessed the scene:

> I only remember the lady on the sidewalk with blood
> all over her. The lady was lying face up. Mrs Dupuis
> was stuffing Kleenex tissues into the gaping hole in the
> abdominal cavity the shotgun made. Another adult who
> I didn't know said, "That won't do any good," but Mrs
> Dupuis just kept stuffing Kleenex into the hole in the
> girl's stomach until all the Kleenex was gone.

Jack was only six years old at the time and the traumatic incident is seared into his memory:

> I'll never forget how the lady's heartbeat was so notice-
> able as she lay there. Every time blood would squirt
> out from her stomach her heart would beat hard – her

chest rising and falling. After so much blood had been lost, her heartbeat became weaker and her chest didn't rise anymore. The ambulance driver arrived and put a compression bandage on her stomach and the little fountains of blood finally stopped.

"I never talked about this to anyone." Jack paused. "But I realize how much it affected me when I retell it now." He continues:

When the excitement died down and my family was all together, we never talked about what happened or how it affected us. As a six-year-old kid, you just dealt with it as best you could. In those days, parents didn't discuss things with their kids the way they do today. That's just how it was.

And where was the young man responsible for this bloodbath? After firing his second shotgun round into Woloch and Ken Chaykoski, Lamb watched his victims scatter. Realizing he had lost control of the situation, he ran across Ford Boulevard while simultaneously breaking open the shotgun, discarding the two smoking empty shell casings, grabbing two more live shells from his pocket, and reloading both barrels and cocking the shotgun—all at a dead sprint, the result of a lifelong fixation with guns.

Grace Dunlop, of 1867 Ford Boulevard, had been enjoying a quiet Saturday evening at home. Nineteen-year-old Dunlop was watching television in her living room, while her fiancé, David Dearsley, was in the kitchen repairing nets and organizing his fishing tackle for an excursion the following day. Like the guests at the Suchius' party, Dearsley heard the two shotgun blasts but dismissed them as firecrackers. Dunlop, however, had second thoughts. Finding the two loud bangs an unusual sound, she decided to take a look outside to investigate. Walking downstairs to the side door that opened onto her driveway, she switched on the exterior light above the open screen door just as Lamb was running up her driveway, fleeing from the bodies lying on the sidewalk directly across the street. Seeing a woman's silhouette in the lighted doorway, Lamb, without hesitating, shot Dunlop through the screen door at near point-blank range. He continued running before disappearing into the darkness of Dunlop's backyard.

Dearsley was almost knocked off his chair as the noise from the shotgun blast bounced off the narrow interior walls of the stairwell up onto the main floor, reverberating throughout the small house. This time the sound was undeniable. Knowing Grace had just walked down the side stairs, he jumped into action. Coming to the stairwell, he gazed down at his bloody and unconscious partner slumped face down on the stairs with pieces of metal screen and wood chips—blown off the door frame—sprinkled over her body. Embedded shotgun pellets and blood splatters marred the interior walls of the stairwell. Neighbours soon entered the side door at the Dunlop house, trying to help Dearsley drag his fiancée upstairs out of the stairwell.

Lehoux and his two sons ran over to see if they could be of assistance. Jack Lehoux recalls the scene: "My dad yelled at us to go home immediately, but not before I saw a crowd of men trying to help drag a woman's body back up the stairwell." His older brother, Michael, added, "You could see the damaged door and door frame from the shotgun shell [...] there was also a lot of blood on the walls."

In the meantime, the killer was on the run. Lamb ran through backyards in a northwesterly direction for two blocks—firing a potshot at a passing car—before appearing again on Westminster Boulevard, a quiet residential street not unlike Ford Boulevard. Walking up the long driveway at 1793 Westminster, Lamb climbed the front porch stairs and banged on the unlocked screen door. Sitting in her living room watching television, Mrs Anne Heaton was startled. She got up and turned on the front porch light to see who could possibly be pounding on her door at this late hour. Upon opening the door, Heaton found a young man standing on her porch cradling what appeared to be a shot-gun or rifle. When asked what he wanted, Lamb told Heaton, "I'm going to shoot you." She quickly turned off the porch light and shut the screen door, but Lamb forced his way in behind her. He then stood just inside the front doorway, his eyes scanning the interior of the Heatons' home without uttering a single word.

Heaton didn't quite know what to make of this young man's peculiar behaviour, quietly standing in her living room, gun in hand. She sensed the intruder had no intention of carry-ing out his threat to shoot her. Despite her fear, she decided to call his bluff, shouting loudly to her husband—sound asleep in a rear bedroom—to call the police and bring his gun to defend her from the armed intruder. Lamb appeared to ignore Heaton's threat, and after a few more minutes had passed, he turned and silently, calmly walked back out the front door. Perplexed, Heaton watched through her front window as the young man lingered at the bottom of the porch steps. Rather than returning toward the street the way he had come, he walked farther up the driveway behind her home. The backyard opened onto a large, undevel-oped field of overgrown weeds and brush, extending west for six hundred metres before ending at Pillette Road, a main roadway and former boundary line between the City of Windsor and the Village of Riverside prior to the merger of the two municipalities earlier that same year.

Heaton, although shaken by her bizarre encounter, decided not to wake her husband as he had a long drive ahead of him the following morning. The family would be leaving to begin their anticipated summer holiday. She decided to retire to bed, making a mental note to tell her husband the next morning about the strange incident with the young man with the gun. Little did she know that Lamb remained in her backyard, implementing a plan he likely formulated on the fly whilst fleeing from his murder rampage on Ford Boulevard.

Lamb took a position, nestling himself down flat on his belly to hide on the opposite side of the crest of a small, grassy hill in the Heatons' backyard. He positioned his rifle with the barrel pointed down the driveway and carefully laid out his live shotgun shells neatly in a row, ready to reload. Now only to wait.

Lamb grew impatient, waiting for the cacophony of sirens and screeching tires coming in to save the day. The police were only two blocks away, hunting for a killer on Ford Boulevard. He was ready. But Anne Heaton did not call the police. Little did she know, but her decision to downplay the standoff in her living room and leave it until morning would thwart Lamb's plans. If police officers had stepped out from their cruisers parked in Heaton's driveway, Lamb would have picked them off like shooting fish in a barrel. Instead, he lay in wait for officers who never showed.

Leaving his shotgun and ammunition behind, Lamb walked west through the open field to Pillette Road, where he flagged a taxi for the short ride back to his uncle's home at 1912 Ford Boulevard. Lamb paid the taxi driver and walked through the front door of his uncle's home, ignoring the emergency vehicles and large crowd gathered outside his residence. Without bothering to change his clothes, Lamb flopped down on his bed and immediately fell into a deep sleep. Less than an hour had passed since he first walked out the door with his uncle's shotgun. Police officers busily gathering evidence at the crime scene would have been stunned to know the killer they sought had walked right past them just up the street.

Immediately following the sidewalk shootings, Windsor patrol officers blockaded the perimeters of the crime scene and began reconstructing the chronology of events amidst the growing chaos, struggling to comprehend what had just transpired outside 1864 Ford Boulevard. Detectives focused on Charmaine Chaykoski, the only uninjured victim who could provide police with a sound physical description of the gunman. The priority for law enforcement at this point was to apprehend the shooter before he could claim more victims. Don Mulesa gave a short statement to the *Windsor Star*, but he and Vincent Franco were generally left on their own, traumatized amidst the frenzied activity and carnage around them. Both young men watched helplessly as ambulances, sirens screaming, drove off with their dying friends.

Senior police officers in black tie and jacket began arriving at the crime scene, having hurriedly left the Windsor Police Awards Night banquet to assist officers at the crime scene. Television and radio news teams from Detroit soon joined them, conducting live interviews while media from as far away as Toronto were racing down Highway 401 to cover the breaking story of multiple shootings by an unknown crazed killer on the loose in Windsor, Ontario.

Throughout the night, uniformed officers and detectives scoured the neighbourhood, searching backyards, garages, any place an armed killer could be hiding. Unfortunately, the police officer in charge of the crime scene on Ford Boulevard failed to order his officers to canvass the neighbours for witnesses with information helpful to the investigation. Mrs Imelda Lehoux of 1886 Ford Boulevard was unable to sleep that night—her nerves shattered—and decided to rest on her front porch. "Police officers walked around our house all night," she recalls, "but no one thought to ask if we knew anything about the shooter. After all, we identified him as Matthew Lamb as soon as he left Hasketh's' house with the gun. We could have saved them a lot of trouble but assumed they knew what they were doing."

Within minutes of the crime, incredulous Windsor residents were informed of shootings in progress on the city's east side. Every weekend, Windsor residents tuned in to CKWW's popular radio talk show "Windsor Speaks," where citizens called in to voice their opinions on local issues with the program's acerbic host. On the night of June 25, 1966, Billy T., a twelve-year-old boy, was sitting with his mother on their front porch listening to talk radio when the show was interrupted by a live bulletin describing ongoing mass shootings. After listening to news updates well into the morning hours, the boy fell asleep only to be awakened shortly thereafter by his father: "That girl who lived next door to us was one of the kids shot. She died this morning!" Jumping out of bed, Billy turned on the radio: "Miss Chaykoski was only twenty years old when doctors pronounced her dead at 5:30 a.m." Edith. His first crush. From that moment, he sensed he would one day become a police officer.

I joined the RCMP shortly after my nineteenth birthday.

CHAPTER THREE:
The Day After

THE FOUR WOUNDED GUNSHOT VICTIMS—
Edith Chaykoski, Andy Woloch, Kenneth Chaykoski, and Grace
Dunlop—arrived in a procession of ambulances at Metropolitan
hospital's emergency room entrance at approximately 10:30
p.m. In 1966, ambulance personnel were not medically trained
as they are today. Their vehicles were converted station wagons
equipped with a siren, a stretcher, a first-aid kit, and a blanket for
warmth to prevent patients from going into shock. Fortunately
for the victims, the hospital was only minutes from the crime
scene. Of the four people shot, only Kenneth Chaykoski was con-
scious upon arrival.

It was almost 1 a.m., early Sunday morning, when Don
Mulesa and Vincent Franco were driven to Metropolitan hospital
to check on the medical conditions of their friends. Just inside
the emergency room entrance, Chaykoski and Woloch lay on
beds separated by a curtain, while nurses rushed back and forth

carrying IVs and bags of blood to Edith's bed, trying to stem her abdominal bleeding. Her condition was so unstable that hospital staff couldn't risk transporting her to the operating theatre. While a surgeon worked on Edith in the triage area, Mulesa and Franco, seated in the waiting room, could hear the doctor's stressed voice calling out commands for blood, sponges, and various medical instruments in a desperate bid to save her life. For the moment, Woloch was hooked up to an IV while medical personnel focused on emergency intervention for Edith.

Grace Dunlop and Kenneth Chaykoski also needed immediate medical attention. At one point the hospital ran out of blood, leading nurses and police officers on duty to volunteer to donate their blood, but even that noble gesture was not enough. With three of the four shooting victims requiring emergency transfusions, Metropolitan hospital ran out of their reserve supplies. Windsor police cruisers raced across town to retrieve special plastic blood containers from the Canadian Red Cross centre— essential for transferring blood from volunteer donors to the gunshot victims. Then Ontario Provincial Police vehicles raced down Highway 401, emergency lights flashing, carrying precious blood from hospitals in London, 160 kilometres northeast of Windsor. Hospital staff made frantic telephone calls from outdated blood donor lists imploring sleepy Windsor residents with matching blood types to help save the lives of the three critically wounded gunshot victims. For the third time that night, police cruisers sped down Windsor's quiet residential streets, now transporting local blood donors—some still in their nightclothes—from their homes to Metropolitan hospital, as Windsor residents pulled together in a collective effort to save these young lives.

The Chaykoski family arrived at the hospital and were met by a nurse who apprised them of Edith's and Kenneth's conditions. The Chaykoskis sat quietly in the ER waiting room, speaking little, each lost in their own thoughts, with the sole exception of an elderly woman weeping quietly. Mrs Edith Chaykoski, mother of the two wounded siblings, struggled to endure the unendurable, unable to see her two children fighting for their lives in a nearby room.

Franco and Mulesa became increasingly worried about Woloch, lying on a stretcher in triage with a tube sticking out of his arm. Peering through the partially opened curtain, they watched a nurse periodically take Woloch's pulse and change his IV bag. Both men fidgeted in their seats, concerned that doctors had forgotten about their friend's abdominal wound. While appreciating the priority given Chaykoski, Franco cannot recall seeing a doctor attend to Woloch during the six hours they spent in the hospital emergency waiting room. Today, Franco suspects that Woloch—being a healthy young athlete in peak physical condition—might have misled doctors to underestimate the gravity of his wounds. Franco and Mulesa badgered exhausted hospital nurses, demanding to know why Andy was not being given adequate medical attention. Agitated medical staff barked back that he was being properly treated, but the two men were unconvinced and remained in the waiting room throughout Sunday morning—unwilling to leave their friend.

At approximately 3 a.m. a haggard-looking physician, wearing a white smock drenched in blood, walked into the waiting room to speak with the Chaykoski family. Family members all jumped to their feet as the doctor approached. "The family," Franco recalls, "was told Edith had stabilized for the moment and that they should go home and get some sleep. The doctor promised to immediately contact them should Edith's condition change." The doctor did have good news about Kenneth Chaykoski. His wounds were not life-threatening and he would completely recover.

Around 5 a.m., Franco vaguely recalls the Chaykoski family rushing back into the hospital again—just two hours after being sent home by the attending physician. Wearing the same bloody smock, the exhausted surgeon explained to Mrs Chaykoski that her daughter had taken a turn for the worse. She would not survive; her internal injuries were too severe. From despair, to hope, then back to despair: the Chaykoskis collectively broke down, devastated by the tragic turn of events. Franco and Mulesa, over-hearing the conversation, quietly pulled the doctor aside and asked if they could see Edith, telling the doctor that "no one should die alone." Their request was denied. Franco's last clear memory of the hospital that Sunday morning was the anguished expressions on the faces of the Chaykoski family. He does not recall what time he and Mulesa left the hospital, but the early-morning sun promised another unbearably hot summer day. The two young men stood outside in the hospital parking lot, disturbed by a nagging awareness their lives had been forever changed.

***

Stanley Hasketh returned home to 1912 Ford Boulevard shortly after 1 a.m. on Sunday stunned by the large crowd standing behind police barricades just outside his home, blocking all access to the block. He had heard radio reports of a shooting in east Windsor, but was unaware of the close proximity of his home to the crime scene. Noting the lights in his house were turned off, Hasketh entered through the rear door while trying to suppress a rising sense of dread in the pit of his stomach. Could his nephew possibly be involved in this tragedy? He tried to dismiss his fear by recalling Lamb's polite mannerisms and diligent work attend-ance since his release from Kingston Penitentiary two weeks earlier. Hasketh later told the media how odd he had thought it was that Lamb always asked permission to use the washroom or take something from the refrigerator, until Lamb explained to his bemused uncle how his behaviour was a conditioned response of his recent incarceration. Hasketh found Lamb's fondness for alcohol somewhat troubling, but had not detected signs of real anger or a propensity for violence—even when Lamb was drink-ing—since Lamb's release from prison.

Walking quietly through to the kitchen and switching on the light, Hasketh immediately noted the empty ammunition box and the shotgun shells strewn across the floor. He ran to the closet where he kept his shotgun. It was not there. With his gun missing and an empty shotgun-shell box sitting on the kitchen table, Hasketh cautiously entered the bedroom where Lamb was sleeping. Nothing if not courageous, he decided to confront his nephew. Gently shaking Lamb awake, Hasketh asked what he knew of the missing shotgun and shells. Initially dodging his uncle's questions, Lamb finally admitted he "was probably responsible for having shot some people." He apologized for any trouble he may have caused his uncle—showing no signs of remorse for any of his victims—then fell back into a deep sleep.

Hasketh knew the police were just outside his front door and considered running out of the house to safety, but he was still unsure of the location of the shotgun. Various nightmare scenarios of what action to take and their possible consequences likely raced through Hasketh's mind. What if Lamb had the loaded shotgun in the house? Was his nephew perhaps testing his uncle's family loyalties? What if Lamb was listening closely and began shooting at Hasketh and his family if they attempted to leave the house? Choosing not to risk the lives of his family or the people congregating outside, Hasketh sat at his kitchen table drinking coffee throughout the night, limiting his movements and longing for daylight when the crowds outside had thinned and he could implement his planned course of action. With the arrival of the sun and Lamb still asleep, Hasketh calmly walked out the door to his car and drove to Tecumseh Road. He hoped that Lamb would not be suspicious as he knew his uncle's morning routine of going out for a newspaper and cup of coffee at a nearby restaurant.

Contacting Windsor Police headquarters from a public telephone Sunday morning, Hasketh was immediately put through to Deputy Chief Ouellette, who had been temporarily leading the as-yet-unassigned investigation into the multiple shootings—now upgraded to a homicide investigation with the confirmed death of Edith Chaykoski earlier that morning. Hasketh told Deputy Chief Ouellette of his nephew's bizarre behaviour when questioned about the missing shotgun and of Lamb's admission. Ouellette convinced Hasketh to immediately drive to police headquarters where the two men devised a plan to arrest Lamb later that day. Hasketh mentioned a pre-planned visit to the assailant's grandmother's house at 2136 York Street, on Windsor's west side, that afternoon. The two men agreed police would knock on the front door at the York Street address at precisely 3 p.m. Hasketh would open the door, allowing police inside the home to arrest Lamb.

Ouellette knew he needed to plan the arrest carefully so as not to compromise the safety of his officers or of innocent civilians inside the home. Ouellette asked Hasketh to draw a layout of the grandmother's home, emphasizing all door and window locations. Ouellette then called Detectives Ken Farrow and Al Boulaine away from their desks and briefed them in his office on the arrest plan, swearing the two detectives to secrecy. Ouellette now had two trusted detectives covering all possible exits but he required a third detective, a man both physically intimidating yet cool-headed in a crisis situation, to do the actual arrest. A police dispatcher sent out a radio call for Detective Sergeant Jim Ure and his partner, Detective Bill Russell, to immediately return to headquarters for briefing. Even then, sensitive information was rarely transmitted over police radios for security reasons, as anyone with the proper equipment can easily monitor police radio transmissions.

Meanwhile, Hasketh had the unenviable task of returning home to 1912 Ford Boulevard where, for the next six hours, he was to keep his naturally suspicious nephew occupied. Lamb was highly intelligent and dangerous—and now a prime murder suspect. Hasketh delivered the acting performance of his life, fully aware he and his wife were the only ones who could directly tie Lamb to the multiple shootings on Ford Boulevard.

Sergeant Frank Chauvin, a lifelong Riverside resident and future recipient of the Order of Canada (our nation's highest civilian award), had reported for duty on the afternoon of the day of the shootings, at the Windsor Police Riverside precinct, then located at Tecumseh Road East and Lauzon Road on Windsor's far east side. Six months earlier, this police precinct had been the headquarters of the Village of Riverside Police Department, but on January 1, 1966, Riverside and four other contiguous municipalities were annexed by the City of Windsor. Like all municipal agencies during this period of expansion and transition, the Windsor Police Department (WPD) was preoccupied and overwhelmed by the difficult task of absorbing five recently independent police departments, each with its own unique operating culture and methods of operation. At the same time, Windsor Police were addressing problems of low officer morale due to poor pay, inadequate training, little public support, and the lingering stigma of past police corruption that had been stamped out by the late 1950s. In that first year of amalgamation, the Windsor Police grew from 245 to 377 police officers and support personnel. Salaries had to be renegotiated, promotion lists revised, municipal legal codes and laws changed to conform to Windsor's bylaws, and a host of other problems dealt with, all of which saw over forty officer resignations in the first two years following the amalgamation.

This was the internal state of affairs when Sergeant Chauvin reported for duty on the steamy afternoon of Saturday, June 25, 1966. As senior shift supervisor, Chauvin, an eleven-year veteran of the now defunct Riverside Police Department, was working the front desk:

> It was shortly after ten on an otherwise quiet Saturday
> night when the police radio exploded with reports of
> multiple shootings in progress in Windsor's east end. As
> senior officer at the detachment, I was always at the duty
> desk. There weren't many cops on the road that night
> because of Awards Night.

The Riverside Precinct was operating with a skeleton crew of patrol officers that night—it was the most important night on the social calendar of every career police officer in the Greater Windsor Area. Awards Night was an annual event sponsored by the City of Windsor, recognizing officers who had distinguished themselves in some capacity the previous year. Moreover, it was the first Awards Night since Windsor's amalgamation with the five new police departments, providing attending officers an opportunity to exchange gossip about imminent policy changes and the potential impact on their careers.

Sergeant Chauvin mostly remembers the stifling heat of that fateful night. Details of the shootings were initially sketchy, so Chauvin called police headquarters and was advised the reports were accurate and a search was currently underway for a young Caucasian male considered armed and extremely dangerous. He was told the case was being handled directly from headquarters downtown and Riverside Precinct would be notified should their assistance be required. Riverside's on-duty squad car—like every other available Windsor Police cruiser—ignored headquarters' instructions and raced to the crime scene to offer assistance and obtain on-scene information to convey to fellow officers back at their respective precincts. By the time Chauvin's shift ended Saturday night, he and his officers knew the basic facts of the shooting rampage involving multiple victims gunned down by an unknown assailant.

Exhausted from working late Saturday night, Chauvin was back at work early the next morning, fulfilling a prior promise to cover the Sunday shift for a fellow officer who had attended the previous night's banquet. The talk in the Riverside Precinct was all about the shootings on Ford Boulevard and the death of Chaykoski announced earlier that morning. Chauvin recalls:

> The case had now been upgraded to a homicide investigation with the death of Chaykoski earlier that morning. Guys [officers] were tossing around names of possible suspects but were unable to think of known violent offenders capable of committing such a baffling crime like this. The apparent lack of motive bewildered officers as it didn't conform to characteristics seen in typical homicide cases.

Police investigators knew how greed, jealousy, revenge, robberies gone bad, and violent domestic disputes led to the vast majority of murders, and had devised strategies and investigative techniques for solving these routine homicides. But the mass shooting of random victims on Ford Boulevard for no apparent reason was a whole new animal—a type of homicide case not seen by Windsor Police detectives prior to 1966.

***

At approximately eight thirty on the Sunday morning following the shootings, Forrest and Anne Heaton pulled out of their driveway at 1793 Westminster Avenue, anxious to begin their long-anticipated summer vacation. After discussing the strange behaviour of the armed young man at their home the night before, Forrest Heaton convinced his spouse to stop and make a police report before proceeding with their trip. Anne Heaton approached Sergeant Chauvin who was working the front desk at the Riverside Precinct. Heaton told Chauvin she didn't think it was a big thing, but at her husband's insistence, she wished to report an odd occurrence at her home the previous evening. She recounted the events of the night before: "There had been a knock at my front door. I turned on the light and opened the screen door for a better look and a young man was on my porch steps holding what appeared to be a rifle or shotgun. When I asked the young man what he wanted, he replied, 'I'm going to shoot you.'" Heaton told Chauvin she tried to quickly close the front door but the young man followed her inside, and stood in her living room. While he did not speak again or make any attempt to shoot her, she was becoming increasingly unnerved as the young man just stood there, looking around her living room for no discernible reason. After telling Chauvin of her bluff, calling out to her husband, she recalled that the young man seemed unbothered, before eventually walking out of the house, up the driveway, and disappearing into the darkness of Heaton's unfenced backyard and the open field beyond.

Chauvin listened to Heaton's story with growing interest. "Are you aware of the shootings which took place two blocks from your home last night about the time this man appeared at your door with a gun?" he asked. "No, I didn't hear anything about that. Neither did my husband." Chauvin told her about the shootings on nearby Ford Boulevard only minutes before the armed stranger appeared on her front porch: "Mrs Heaton's face went pale when she realized her description of the armed young man at her home matched the physical description of the shooter. I told her he was likely the 'shotgun killer' every police agency in Southwestern Ontario was actively seeking."

Chauvin took a formal statement from Heaton and suggested she postpone her vacation until case detectives had an opportunity to speak with her. Deeply shaken, she left a contact number while Chauvin immediately called his superiors at headquarters to report Heaton's strange encounter with the likely murder suspect, still at large. Chauvin was not told of Hasketh's interview with Deputy Chief Ouellette earlier that Sunday morning, or of the plan to arrest a key suspect later that afternoon. He was, however, ordered to forward to police headquarters a copy of his police occurrence report of the incident, together with Heaton's written statement for investigative follow-up.

What transpired next has never been made public. Chauvin acted on a hunch and dispatched a police cruiser to check the area around the Heatons' home for any possible evidence that could tie the armed intruder to the shootings on Ford Boulevard:

> Within minutes, our guys found a loaded double-barrelled shotgun placed on the opposite side of a small hill in the Heatons' backyard...behind this small hill they found the shotgun and five or six live shotgun shells lined up in a row, placed within easy reach for a shooter to quickly reload the weapon. It was obvious someone had been lying there in the grass and was just waiting to ambush the cops when they arrived at the Heaton home.

Moreover, concealing the shotgun on the opposite slope of the hill provided ideal defensive cover for a shooter with a clear line of fire down the Heatons' driveway. Had police been immediately summoned, police cars would have raced to Anne Heaton's home from the Ford Boulevard crime scene just two streets away. Police officers would've walked up the driveway to the front porch, placing themselves directly in the gunsights of a shooter lying unseen in the darkness beyond the Heaton residence. Chauvin summarized the significance surrounding the murder weapon:

> Riverside officers, after retrieving the shotgun and shells, were aghast at the implications of the shooter's clear intent to ambush police officers responding to a call from Mrs Heaton–a call she fortunately chose not to make." Her decision to wait until the following day to report the incident had wrecked Lamb's plans to shoot police officers in a glorious firefight, likely to end in "death by cop" (DBC)—a grand finale to Lamb's Saturday-night murder rampage.

The shotgun and ammunition were taken to the Riverside Police Detachment, bagged and tagged, and delivered to police headquarters downtown that same Sunday morning, along with Chauvin's occurrence report and Heaton's written statement. Chauvin made a point of including in his official report how the shotgun and ammunition had been found behind the Heaton home, stating his conviction that the evidence revealed the assailant's intent to shoot anyone arriving at the Heaton residence. Rumours of the thwarted ambush of police officers spread quickly through police channels, although the media never got wind of it or, if they did, they failed to follow up on the story.

It doesn't take much investigative skill to realize Lamb had no intention of shooting Heaton. Having just shot four people two streets away, Lamb had no compunction about killing more. Rather, intending to scare Heaton just enough, Lamb would reasonably have expected her to immediately call the police once he left her home. He set up his golden opportunity to kill police officers—always the prime target of his violent fantasies—from behind his hastily built sniper's nest in the Heatons' backyard. The large open field behind the home also provided a perfect escape route.

***

Former Windsor Police Inspector Jim Ure is a physically imposing man. Standing six feet five and weighing 240 pounds, Ure fills a room in much the same way trained actors do, unconsciously sucking up the oxygen from the room and radiating a self-confidence only enhanced by a baritone voice honed to intimidating perfection over thirty-five years of police work. Today, at ninety, Ure remains an impressive figure despite the rigors of old age. In police jargon, Ure was a "cop's cop" or "door kicker": highly valued by fellow officers for deterring local punks from "testing their luck." Ure joined the department in 1949, assigned to the "morality squad"—comparable to today's vice squads. The morality squad's focus was on gambling, prostitution, and bootlegging (the illegal selling of alcohol in unlicensed commercial and residential establishments commonly known by their street names—blind pigs).

Ure joined the WPD at a time of rampant corruption within the police force. The scandal first came to public attention on March 8, 1950, during a judgment read out in open court by Magistrate J. A. Hanrahan during the sentencing of Joe Assef, Windsor's most successful bootlegger at the time. After sentencing Assef to six months in jail, Hanrahan commented on the "laxity" in the WPD for having allowed Assef to operate a criminal enterprise that had pulled off 5,400 deliveries of illegal alcohol in two months. The rebuke set off an immediate firestorm within the WPD that, by 1952, had resulted in the resignations of Windsor Police Chief Claude Renaud, Deputy Chief W. H. Neale, and the firing of numerous police officers—ironically including many of Ure's peers in the morality squad.

Ure, in 1950, a rookie on the morality squad, recalls the internal investigations of Windsor Police officers and of the unacknowledged hero of the WPD responsible, more than anyone else, for cleaning up corruption within the department:

> When this whole story broke, Inspector John Burns was put in charge of the morality squad. Burns, a farm boy like me, came from a family well-known for its criminal activities. But John was different. He was straitlaced and a workaholic who fired anyone with even a taint of corruption. Most compromised officers took payoffs in free liquor. Burns even had his own son arrested, commenting to other officers that "his boy's criminality should've 'gotten him killed'." When the OPP appointed Carl Farrow—a legend in the [Toronto headquarters of the OPP]—as the new Windsor police chief in 1951, Farrow promoted Burns to deputy chief of the WPD. Burns retired as deputy chief, but with the small pension even senior officers received, he didn't get the entitlements or recognition he deserved.

The termination of rank-and-file police officers involved in corruption would continue unabated throughout the 1950s. By 1958, the WPD had been thoroughly "cleaned up" and structural changes introduced to professionalize the police department. Standardized written tests now became mandatory for all police applicants. Furthermore, police experience and aptitude became prime factors in the hiring and promotion of officers. Traditional nepotism as a principal feature in the hiring of WPD officers was abolished.

Years after the Lamb spree killings, Ure and Officer Tim Copeland would jointly arrest the killer of Charlie Brooks, co-founder of the Canadian Auto Workers Union (CAW), and one of the most powerful and beloved labour leaders in Canada. In 1977, Brooks was shot dead with a high-powered rifle in his Windsor office by a recently fired auto worker who blamed Brooks for Chrysler's refusal to rehire him. The assassin was fleeing the scene, rifle in hand, as Ure coincidentally happened to be driving by CAW headquarters, unaware of the shooting that had just occurred. The killer, recognizing Ure from past arrests, quietly placed his rifle on the ground and lay face down on the pavement while Officer Copeland handcuffed the suspect. The assassin was subsequently charged and convicted for Brooks's murder. Jim Ure just had that kind of effect on criminals.

On early Sunday morning, June 26, 1966, Ure and Detective Bill Russell were walking through the field behind 1793 Westminster Avenue searching for any evidence left behind by the intruder following Lamb's confrontation with Anne Heaton. Both officers were unaware the shotgun used in the Ford Boulevard shootings had already been found that morning behind the Heaton home and a suspect identified. Ure explains what happened next:

> I don't remember the exact time of day, but I remember the terrible, hot, hot, humid weather was already unbearable. We were walking through that field in back of Westminster Boulevard when my partner said, "You know, Jim, somebody is going to call us on this one. It is such a bizarre crime." Not three minutes later, a call came over our radio. We were called in and instructed to arrest a suspect for the shootings at a house over on York Street.

At 3 p.m. precisely, Ure knocked on the front door at 2136 York Street. Crouched beneath the windows on the east and west sides of the home were Detectives Ken Farrow and Al Boulaine. Stanley Hasketh answered the knock at the front door as planned with police earlier that day, and Ure walked into the living room. "Lamb was sitting quietly on a recliner, shirtless and perspiring from the heat, drinking a beer as he watched television. He was as calm as could be, quietly listening as I told him he was under arrest on suspicion of the murder of Edith Chaykoski and wounding of three others."

Unaware of the prearranged arrest, Lamb's grandmother was near hysterical as she suddenly found herself staring down the barrel of a .38-calibre snub-nose revolver held by Detective Fred Stuart, who stormed into her home through the back door just as Ure was calmly informing Lamb of his arrest in the front living room. Someone at police headquarters had obviously leaked information about the planned arrest of the suspected shotgun killer. Police cars converged from all directions on the York street home to provide unwanted backup just as Ure walked through the front door to arrest Lamb. "It became something of a farce," Ure laughingly recalls. "I was just talking to the guy [Lamb] without any problems when fellow detectives started swarming into the house from every direction. Anyway, I handcuffed Lamb and took him downtown without any further incident." Lamb was booked, photographed, fingerprinted, and a "charge statement" for the crime of capital murder completed and read back to Lamb in accordance with Canadian law. Lamb declined to give Ure—now designated the lead investigator in the Lamb spree killings—a statement regarding his actions the previous evening. Lamb was then taken to a holding cell to await a court appearance the following day when formal charges would be laid.

Ure next interviewed Mrs Anne Heaton at her home on Westminster, where Heaton reiterated the details of her strange confrontation with Lamb the night before, as told earlier that morning to Sergeant Chauvin at the WPD Riverside detachment. Unfortunately, the precise details of how the shotgun was discarded and found by Riverside Police officers were not brought to Ure's attention at the time—a costly communicative slip-up of considerable consequence for the future capital murder charge filed against Lamb.

In every interview conducted with detectives involved in the Lamb spree killings, a curious manifestation arose that deserves telling. I first noted it while interviewing Inspector Jim Ure about the Lamb murder spree. Ure was relating details of the Lamb case when he suddenly stopped speaking mid-sentence. A fixed gaze appeared on his expressionless face, as if he was reliving or trying to recall the sequence of events. Ure then remarked:

"God, she was a beautiful young woman."

"Edith Chaykoski?" I asked.

"What? Oh no," Ure replied. "I was just remembering a case I had in the 1970s where a girl was shot dead in her living room over a silly domestic dispute with the neighbours upstairs. I don't know if you want to get into this or not."

While digging in his psyche to recollect the details of the Lamb case, Ure had triggered memories of a different homicide from the same era. He seemed to want to unburden himself, so I encouraged him to continue to talk about this unrelated murder case, so he was encouraged to go on with his story. The case was one of numerous homicides Ure investigated over the years, but something about this particular murder still bothered him some forty-five years later:

> Well, this girl, from a nice family, I can't remember the names or the year, sometime in the early seventies, I think. She had a problem with her neighbours upstairs that got out of hand. The husband had an altercation with the upstairs neighbour's boyfriend, or one of them anyway, so these hoods upstairs called for help from some unsavory Drouillard Road guys whose idea of help was to drive over and shoot up the downstairs apartment where this girl and her husband lived. It was winter and the curtains had been drawn on the front window. In a sudden burst of gunfire through that front window, one random bullet struck this girl in the head,

killing her almost instantly... What a waste! We knew
who the killer was but could never get anybody to talk.

Two weeks after this interview, while taking photos of Ure in his
back garden for this book, the same thing happened. Ure shook
his head, whispering to himself: "She was just such a beautiful
young girl." He then apologized for talking to himself. "Sorry, I
was just thinking of this case I had years ago where this beautiful
young girl took a bullet in the head over a stupid argument with a
fellow tenant." Ure had obviously forgotten our earlier conversation about this particular homicide, but it was the first appearance
of the Lawman's Ghost. Years later, these police officers were still
carrying these cases around with them, unable to mentally file
away the details. Ure remains haunted by the living spirit of one
of the many long-dead innocent victims one routinely encounters
in police work.

The homicide case troubling Ure was the murder of Silvanna
Wild (née DeSantis), a young wife and mother who resided at
1016 Pelissier Street in Windsor's upper downtown district. Mrs
Wild and her husband, a local author, were on bad terms with
the upstairs neighbour who was known to have small-time criminal connections. The dispute escalated to the point where, on the
night of December 12, 1972, bullets were fired from the front yard
of 1016 Pelissier Street through the front window of the Wilds'
ground-floor apartment. Silvanna was struck in the head and
fell to the floor, mortally wounded, in the presence of her sister,
mother, and her two young children. She succumbed later that
evening to a .38-calibre bullet wound to the head. Ure was placed
in charge of the investigation the following day.

Ure's first task was to attend Wild's autopsy to retrieve
bullet fragments and any other pertinent evidence for forensic
analysis at the Toronto Crime Laboratory. Case officers are legally
required to take personal possession of all key evidence to prove
"continuity of possession." This is a standard but necessary legal
requirement to prevent defence lawyers from later arguing that

evidence produced in court was contaminated from being handled by persons other than the case officer and forensic personnel assigned to the case. The mandatory police attendance at forensic autopsies is experienced differently by individual police officers. Autopsies performed on children or innocent victims of foul play are always difficult as the process can unintentionally dehumanize them as people. Police officers witness the pain inflicted on grieving family members for loved ones murdered by violent criminals. Having to watch a pathologist methodically dismember the subject of a family's grief is a psychological barrier that all police investigators have to cross and accept as a necessary part of the job. Whether personally affected by Silvanna Wild's autopsy, or plagued by frustration over his inability to charge Wild's killer, nothing identifiable explains *why* this particular case stands out amongst the numerous homicide cases Ure has investigated throughout a long career. I suspect Ure himself does not know the answer—only that it haunts him forty-five years after the event and will do so for the rest of his days. That is the mystery and the tragedy of the Lawman's Ghost.

***

Lamb's shooting rampage on the night of June 25, 1966, had terrible consequences that still resonate over fifty years later. Edith Chaykoski was dead. Andrew Woloch lay fighting for his life in Metropolitan hospital together with Kenneth Chaykoski, the latter recovering from gunshot wounds to his right arm and hip by the same shotgun blast that felled Woloch. Grace Dunlop had been severely injured. Had some of the shotgun pellets embedded in the door frame and stairwell walls of the Dunlop residence struck their intended target she likely would not have survived. Lamb's cruelty cost Dunlop a kidney, but the young woman would eventually recover. Charmaine Chaykoski was placed under a doctor's care for treatment of trauma and concern for her advanced state of pregnancy.

On Wednesday, June 29, 1966, Edith Chaykoski was buried in St. Alphonsus Cemetery, one of Windsor's oldest Catholic grave-yards. A modest, flat concrete gravestone slowly receding into the ground by the forces of time and gravity marks Chaykoski's final resting place. Her grave is located in the cemetery's children's section, where gravestones recording short time intervals between birth and death testify to lives unnaturally cut short for reasons unstated—stone epitaphs written in tears. Dead at the young age of twenty, Chaykoski had been blessed with a longer life than most of the children buried around her. It is a scene that evokes an emotional response where one can envision Chaykoski's spirit eternally watching over the souls of her younger charges with the same compassion and vigilance she had shown toward her elderly nursing home patients in life.

Tragedy also pursued the physically unharmed victims of Lamb's vicious rampage. On June 27, 1966, two days after the Saturday-night massacre, an article in the *Windsor Star* thoughtlessly posed the question as to why Don Mulesa and Vincent Franco, the two men unhurt in the shooting spree, failed to attack Lamb after the second shot was fired. The article states: "Due to shock, neither of the two unwounded boys thought to rush the gunman after both barrels of the shotgun had been discharged. He [Lamb] apparently reloaded on the run before encountering the girl." The obvious inference is that Dunlop would not have been shot and seriously wounded had Franco and Mulesa immediately attacked Lamb following the second shotgun blast, which struck Andy Woloch and Kenneth Chaykoski. This *Windsor Star* columnist caused these two young men endless grief that Franco admits still bothers him to this day. These two men had no idea what kind of gun Lamb used during the attack as neither man was knowledgeable about firearms. Moreover, Lamb's firing at six pedestrians in a confrontation lasting about thirty seconds was completely unexpected. Many police officers trained in the use of firearms would not have had the presence of mind to rush the shooter in similar circumstances. The *Windsor*

Star also couldn't get its facts straight, misstating that Charmaine Chaykoski and her wounded husband "ran *across the street* [italics added] to seek help from the merrymakers" at the Suchius' garage party. The *Star* reporter responsible for this article was ignorant of the fact Lamb's attack occurred on the public sidewalk directly *in front* of the Suchius' garage party—not across the street. The reporter likely hadn't even bothered to visit the crime scene. Yet the damage was done.

Unfortunately for Franco and Mulesa, Windsor residents in 1966 relied on the *Windsor Star* as their primary source of information about the shooting spree, and a few ignorant and malicious souls found satisfaction in verbally attacking the survivors. When Franco reported for work on Tuesday, just three days after the shootings, one co-worker laughingly told Franco that "it should have been you that was killed." Employees berated him for failing to attack Lamb after the second shotgun blast, parroting the *Star* article. One day shortly after the shooting rampage, Franco and Mulesa were sitting on the latter's front porch grieving for their dead and wounded friends, drinking a beer in the sweltering heat to help calm their shattered nerves. Mrs Suchiu, hostess of the anniversary garage party where the sidewalk shooting spree occurred, walked past the two men, then stopped, turned, and began scolding Franco: "You know, you knocked two beer bottles off my porch the other night and I had to pick up all the glass from that bottle you broke. Somebody could have seriously cut themselves." She was referring to the empty beer bottle Franco took from her side porch to protect himself while assisting his dying friends bleeding out on the sidewalk in front of the Suchiu residence. Stunned by this woman's verbal abuse and misplaced priorities, Franco and Mulesa said nothing, struggling to understand the lack of compassion and incomprehensible logic of Mrs Suchiu a long-time neighbour and wife of a local minister.

As the days passed, the world increasingly made less sense to the two young men. Franco's mother insisted they visit Woloch's mother to offer their encouragement and support for her still hospitalized son. Mrs Woloch answered the knock at her door, instantly recognizing Franco and his mother, but wearing a stern, guarded face usually reserved for unwanted solicitors. Mrs Franco was offering the requisite sympathies to Mrs Woloch, expressing hope for her son's quick recovery, when Woloch angrily snapped: "Sure, but it wasn't your son that was shot, was it?"—before slamming the door shut on Franco and his mother.

This lack of empathy and misplaced anger directed at the survivors by friends, co-workers, and neighbours was palpable yet difficult to explain. It was likely rooted in a collective fear, particularly among the residents of Ford Boulevard. Their rudeness masked a deeply felt, and previously unknown, sense of vulnerability following Lamb's violent intrusion into the banal familiarities of their neighbourhood that once held the outside world at bay—a collective mourning for a sense of security lost forever. Lamb's shooting spree echoed similarly through neighbourhoods across Windsor and beyond. The emergence of a "rampage killer" was a terrifying and incomprehensible anomaly in 1966—unlike today when spree killings and sadistic crimes are routine events shamefully accepted as part of popular culture.

Several days following the shootings, Franco and Mulesa attempted to visit their close friend Andy Woloch, still recovering in Metropolitan hospital. Through the open door of Woloch's hospital room, they saw their friend sitting up in bed, reading from a stack of engineering textbooks strewn about his hospital bed. Same old Andy, Franco thought, already preparing for the upcoming fall semester at the University of Windsor. Woloch failed to notice his two best friends standing in the doorway before a nurse quickly pulled Franco and Mulesa away and escorted them off the floor, admonishing them for breaching a restricted area of the hospital.

Two days after Franco and Mulesa's aborted visit and seventeen days following Lamb's shotgun blast to his stomach, Andrew Woloch died unexpectedly. The coroner's report found an undetected abscess behind Woloch's liver that had become infected, triggering further complications and resulting in the young man's death. Magnetic resonance imaging (MRI), computerized axial tomography (CAT) scans, and ultrasound diagnostics did not exist in 1966. Detective Sergeant Jim Ure believes—with good reason—that Woloch would have survived had today's technology then been available. Franco, however, remains convinced Woloch would have survived his injuries had he undergone immediate surgery upon arrival at the hospital on the night of the shootings, instead of languishing for hours on an emergency room table, alone and unattended. Whatever the truth, Lamb bears sole responsibility for Woloch's death.

The two-year consecutive scoring star of the University of Windsor's hockey team and honour student in the Faculty of Engineering would be posthumously honoured with a front-page photo and biography in the University of Windsor's 1966–67 yearbook.

Woloch was buried in Heavenly Rest Catholic Cemetery, an immense and immaculately maintained graveyard just outside Windsor's municipal boundary. Each section of the graveyard is guarded by a large stone sculpture of one of heaven's archangels. Andrew lies in the section overseen by the Archangel Gabriel. Engraved on a marble headstone are three names: those of Mr and Mrs Woloch and their only child, Andrew Woloch, dead at the age of twenty-one. The parents outlived their son by many years, forced to cope daily with the loss of their only child, their pride and joy. In one senseless act, Matthew Charles Lamb had destroyed an entire family.

News of Andrew's death was printed prominently in the *Windsor Star* on July 12, 1966. Two days later, another terrible headline was emblazoned across the front page: 8 DEAD IN THE CRIME OF THE CENTURY. Chicago had been rocked by a gruesome, also seemingly random crime as eight nurses were murdered by a stranger. We know him today as the infamous Richard Speck.

The summer of 1966—Windsor and the rest of the world would never be the same.

CHAPTER FOUR:
A New Kind of Killer

THE PUBLIC'S PERCEPTION OF VIOLENT CRIME could not be more different today than it was in the summer of 1966. Lamb's spree shocked the nation and disrupted the humdrum of Windsor's blue-collar lifestyle. What happened? Canadian homicide rates are virtually the same today as they were then. In fact, 1966 was the last year for low homicide rates in the postwar era, with an average of 1.28 homicides per 100,000 residents. What followed was a steady, dramatic increase that peaked in 1975 at 3.08—the nation's highest ever recorded homicide rate—before settling into a downward trend to contemporary homicide rates. The United States mirrored Canada during this period, with low rates until 1966 and a similar spike in the mid-1970s. Homicide has recently increased in Canada from 1.44 per 100,000 in 2013 to 1.8 per 100,000 in 2018—which research suggests is the direct result of increased organized gang activity in major cities. This, however, is dramatically short of the nation's 1975 rate or even of the smaller increases in the 1990s. What did change? This era saw the birth of the modern news cycle, changing society's relationship to violent crimes forever.

Throughout the 1960s, North American families received their news from local television or print newspapers. Introduction of the television set added an element of drama and shared experience that far surpassed that of its predecessor—the radio—as a public forum. By 1960, even people of the most modest means owned a small-screen black-and-white television set—broadcasting 1.5 hours of local, national, and international news per twenty-four-hour cycle, condensed into three segments of thirty minutes each, aired at noon, 6 p.m., and 11 p.m. National newspapers such as the *New York Times* or Canada's *Toronto Star* scarcely sold outside of major cities. The major American television networks such as ABC, NBC, and CBS, along with the CBC in Canada were heavily regulated and formatted to present the news in a straightforward manner without editorial comment. The news was to operate as a public service, an accepted money-losing operation for otherwise profitable networks, where entertainment and news were deigned never to meet. "The 'church' of news was to be separated from the 'state' of entertainment," in the words of communications expert Daniel Hallin. The policy of major networks in the early 1960s was to cede crime stories to local media outlets, unless the circumstances of the crime were of an exceptional nature deemed in the public interest. As opposed to the big networks, for local television stations "news" was big money, alone constituting 50 to 60 percent of a station's profits. It was the local stations that allowed a "heavy entertainment-oriented form of programming to evolve," leaving a poorly informed public to negatively contrast the limited information told by "poker-faced network anchors" with the more detailed and visually satisfying coverage provided by local stations.

By the mid-1960s, however, high Nielsen ratings and increasing advertising revenue for local channels had caught the eyes of corporate executives who saw these ratings as untapped

revenue waiting to be made. Massive profits were just too important to leave to journalists. As network news became increasingly
subject to intense media competition, well-researched topics
and news documentaries offering unique perspectives on problems, policies, and controversial issues were replaced with softer
stories on celebrities, personal health, and lifestyles. Television
news focused on personal, not public, life—beginning their slow
descent into their current role as adjuncts to the media/enter-
tainment complex, mixing fact, speculation, and entertainment
into news narratives. By today's standards, the consumer of the
1960s was very limited in the amount of information received, yet
viewed network news with a far less critical eye than we do now.

As we just learned, crime rates took off from 1966 and the
media was right there to cover it. By the early 1970s, the over-
reporting of rare, sensationalist murders that both shocked and
fascinated became a major topic for the media and news maga-
zine shows such as *60 Minutes,* followed by spinoff news shows
that mixed fact with spectacle, such as *A Current Affair, Hard
Copy,* and *Inside Edition*—a victory for "tabloid journalism."
Hollywood contributed with a multitude of television police
dramas and films casting anti-hero serial killers, spree killers,
lust killers, thrill killers and other mass murderers; supplemented
by numerous books and magazines, both fiction and non-fiction,
with violent crime narratives. Mass murder—of avid interest to
the news media and Hollywood had, as early as 1969, become a
primary motive for many killers eager to indulge in their lurid
activities for the media attention and fear their crimes invoked.
Popular culture made mass murderers and particularly serial killers infamous—a fate many twisted criminals would embrace to
attain their fifteen minutes of fame. The still-at-large serial killer
known as Zodiac terrorized San Francisco in the summer of 1969,
initiating a cat-and-mouse game with law enforcement, sending
coded letters to the media requesting people wear "I like Zodiac"
buttons on their shirts or "he might get sad and kill again." While
San Francisco detectives worked double shifts in search of the

Zodiac, actor Clint Eastwood became an international star in his role as Detective Harry Callahan of the San Francisco Police, immortalizing this elusive serial killer in the hit film *Dirty Harry*.

The Manson family's 1969 home invasion massacres of the Tate and LaBianca families of Hollywood became an international media sensation, portraying the diminutive schemer and ex-con Charles Manson as both a Svengali and a hippie Antichrist—in the process driving a knife through the heart of 'hippie flower power and an increasingly discredited 1960s counterculture. The 1970s saw serial murderers such as Houston, Texas, native Dean Corll, aka the Candy Man, who paid two local teenagers to bring him new victims, then sexually assaulted, tortured, murdered, and buried at least twenty-eight young Houston boys from 1969 to 1972, a crime that shocked and fascinated North Americans after it was detailed in the bestselling 1974 book *Mass Murder in Houston*, whose title illustrates how the term *serial killer* had not yet entered the vernacular of popular culture. These serial murders were soon overshadowed by the West Coast's Ted Bundy, aka the Deliberate Stranger; New York's David Berkowitz, aka the Son of Sam; Richard Ramirez, aka the Night Stalker, who terrified Los Angeles with a spate of brutal killings; John Wayne Gacy, aka the Killer Clown, from Chicago; and Dennis Rader of Wichita, Kansas, aka BTK (bind, torture, kill)—just a few of the prolific American serial killers who generated international media interest throughout the 1970s. Like the Zodiac, both Berkowitz and Rader communicated with the media as a means of enhancing their murderous status and generating more fear within their communities. Rader contacted police soon after slaughtering the four members of the Otero family in 1974, complaining, "How many people do I have to kill before I get my name in the paper or some national media attention?"

Detailed public information on sensationalist murders of the late 1960s was to be found in "true detective magazines," with their lurid covers featuring helpless, frightened women in bondage and poorly written narratives, perched high on the top shelf at the local drugstore. Mass murder was indeed newsworthy, yet the television news media's growing penchant for story selectivity for emotional impact to attract viewership helped create a warped perspective of violence and its social impact on viewers. On a positive note, the media has recently played a more constructive role, supporting such initiatives as Amber Alerts that seek the help of the general public in finding missing children, and also alert the public to general dangers, and television shows such as *America's Most Wanted*, whose format is designed to educate and warn the public and identify violent criminals still at large.

In 1966, however, this framework was only beginning. The news media's fascination with violent, sensationalized crime was virtually non-existent—unlike today, when the public is often oversaturated and desensitized from a barrage of news from multiple platforms. If society in the early 1960s was unprepared for the rise of violent, sadistic crimes that were to come, what of law enforcement?

***

It is a paradox that in 1966—the year with the lowest homicide rates in Canada and the United States—the general public witnessed reports of widely publicized mass murderers, foretelling the coming of the new types of killers that would, and continue to, challenge law enforcement. What had forensic science understood about mass murder in the early 1960s? Various academic studies prior to 1966 show the available research was rudimentary but instructive—if not yet disseminated to police agencies or the general public.

Early forensic studies cited in *The American Journal of Psychiatry* focused on the *motive* of rational, coherent, and intelligent men who committed irrational crimes usually associated with the "insane murderer." One 1960 study of five men in this category concluded all five were sane and not suffering from "psychosis—causing delusions or hallucinations"—they rather "were

49

fully aware of what they were doing and knew their actions were wrong" when committing their crimes. The murderers were themselves baffled by their own horrific acts, all multiple homicides, and spoke of having experienced a sense of being in a dreamlike, dissociative state at the time, feeling as if someone else was committing the crimes while consciously aware they were the person responsible. A significant finding confirmed these killers had a lifelong history of erratic control over aggressive impulses and a history of frequent involvement in violent fights that were not typical altercations—but "fights that could have easily escalated to homicide had they not been restrained by others." These men all had poor ego-perceptions of themselves as inferior or inadequate men. Each had been raised in a violent and chaotic family environment while subjected to physical, sexual, and/or mental abuse during childhood. In all cases, there was evidence of "severe emotional deprivation" early in life, in which "one or both parents were unknown or outright rejected the child."

Furthermore, none of the murderers involved in the study experienced anger or rage while committing their brutal crimes or showed any sign of empathy, guilt about, or remorse for their victims following their arrests and convictions. Typically, their relationships with others were of a shallow nature, increasing the isolation and loneliness of these men from other people whom they saw as "mere props" in their own personal life dramas. These men displayed all the signs of extreme narcissism typical of the psychopathic personality, and having suffered early and intense damage to their self-esteem, compensated by a delusional, grandiose conception of themselves. They responded with violent rage when their inflated self-image was believed to be under attack. These men were psychoanalytically and legally sane, well aware, while committing their crimes, that their actions were wrong. Yet, the study of personality profiles and behaviours of "violent murders without motive" by "psychopathic" killers was still a relatively unexplored field in 1960, followed by intensive research later in the decade in response to increasing homicide rates.

Over the last fifty years, law enforcement has painstakingly developed terminology to classify behavioural traits of mass murderers in response to the rising phenomenon of what the FBI called "mass murders without motive"—baffling crimes that demanded a different approach to criminal forensics. Terms such as *spree killer, serial killer,* and *rampage killer* were non-existent; all these men were classified as "mass murderers" at the time. Specific nomenclature to distinguish between types of mass killers were the product of the FBI's Behavioural Science Unit in the early 1970s. Together with *forensic psychiatry,* these terms helped to codify specific behavioural traits of offenders who commit mass murder, allowing law enforcement to narrow suspect lists and better understand the psychology and motives of criminals who commit multiple homicides. These are not legal or medical terms and are primarily of interest to law enforcement and an intrigued popular culture.

Mass murder is generally defined as four or more murders occurring during one continuous period of time, with no distinctive time period between the murders. However tragic, mass murder is usually a one-off event. Mass murderers also show a wide variance in their choice of victims. They may target family members, people in workplaces or schools, or random victims who present themselves as targets of opportunity. Matthew Lamb's shooting spree in Windsor, Ontario; Richard Speck's 1966 massacre of eight student nurses in Chicago; Charles Whitman's premeditated shooting spree from the Bell Tower at the University of Texas at Austin in 1966; James Huberty's 1984 McDonald's massacre in San Ysidro, California; and the 1999 Columbine school shooting rampage by students Dylan Klebold and Eric Harris are well-cited examples of mass murderers who paved the way for the copycat killers that followed.

Spree killing is generally defined as the murder of two or more people at more than one location, without a cooling-off period in between for the offender. The maximum duration between kills is generally accepted to be seven days. Spree killers do not trouble themselves with the consequences of their crimes, as up to 80 per-cent are estimated to be suicidal at the time they commit them, accepting beforehand that they will either be killed by police, com-mit suicide, or surrender upon completing their killing spree. They may or may not know their victims but seem to exhibit a larger degree of randomness in their choice of target than serial killers or other mass killers. Their killing occurs while in a state of personal mobility, their crimes less methodical and organized than those of "mission-oriented" mass murderers like Charles Whitman.

The "mass murderer or spree killer" argument is ongoing for academics and criminologists, many of whom advocate elimin-ating the category of spree killer altogether, as there is too much overlap with the mass murderer designation. Law enforcement generally ignores the debate as the two definitions do not impede investigative procedures or hasten crime resolution. *Rampage killers* is a convenient term applied to spree killers who claim an unusually large number of victims, usually ten or more. One widely shared trait common to spree, rampage, and serial killers when committing their crimes is the "God complex," a type of euphoria or "high" experienced while killing—a desire to hold ultimate power over life and death and be further rewarded with a feeling of intense calm and purged rage following their kills. This power/reward ratio is a key motivating factor admitted to by many mass murderers, spree killers, and serial killers.

Spree shootings with high casualties have substantially increased in the first two decades of the twenty-first century, even as serial murders have been in long-term decline for this same period, a statistical fact that should be—and recently has become—of increasing interest to criminologists and other social scientists. Shootings in schools and shopping malls, or in other public places, draw a media firestorm as these crimes often strike the most vul-nerable: children. The mostly young, troubled men engaging in this type of mass murder have today supplanted the serial killer as the most feared violent criminal in the public consciousness.

Serial killer is defined as one who claims three or more victims, all murdered in separate locations at different times. Serial killers are usually quite selective in their choice of victims—unlike most mass murderers or spree killers—and plan their crimes more carefully as they do not wish to be caught. Serial killers can operate for years within one geographical area, such as BTK in Wichita, Kansas, or alternatively, like Tommy Lynn Sells, a prolific serial killer who travelled throughout the United States on railroad freight cars and claimed to have killed seventy people over a twenty-year period. What differentiates serial killers from mass murderers is the characteristic "cooling off" period, an emotional hiatus from the anger, anxiety, and overwhelming compulsion that consumes them prior to each murder, allowing these killers to decompress and resume a normal lifestyle after a fresh kill—thus making their capture all the more difficult.

There is one more important piece to the puzzle for law enforcement—one that cops in 1966 were entirely unprepared to face. In the years since, forensic psychiatry and crime analysis have identified the psychopathic mind as central to the problem and seek to understand the condition and, more important, to answer this question: Can psychopathy be successfully treated?

Psychopathy is a baffling personality disorder common to mass murderers and a major factor in recidivist violent crime, imposing a significant burden on our criminal justice system. According to a 2012 FBI report, a psychopath bears a "cluster of interpersonal affective, lifestyle, and antisocial traits and behaviours." This includes "deception; manipulation; irresponsibility; impulsivity; stimulation seeking; poor behavioural controls; lack of empathy, guilt, or remorse; sexual promiscuity; callous disregard for the rights of others; and unethical and antisocial behaviours." It's nature and nurture at play to create a psychopath: their biology and temperament but also social forces and upbringing. The result? Psychopaths operate in a "cold-blooded manner, using people as pawns to achieve goals and satisfy their needs and desires." In other words, they lack the mechanism of shame or a moral compass—there's no conscience.

Psychopaths have always been with us. You can find hints of them in the records of pre-industrial societies. Theophrastus, a student of Aristotle, called them the *unscrupulous*. According to Katherine Ramsland, Inuit call psychopaths *kunlangeta* for those "whose mind knows what to do but he does not do it."

One characteristic all serial killers, and many spree killers, share is antisocial personality disorder (ASPD). ASPD is the equivalent medical definition for psychopathy, a condition not recognized in the *Diagnostic and Statistical Manual of Mental Disorders* (DSM). The main difference is that ASPD is more broad—psychopathy is determined in a criminal justice setting through a checklist of items, whereas ASPD is medically diagnosed through behavioural study. The FBI accepts this clinical definition for psychopathy and, likewise, the DSM acknowledges that ASPD is often referred to as psychopathy. Put simply, all psychopaths have ASPD, but the reverse is not always true. Psychopathy is gender neutral—although psychopathic men are still more likely to resort to violence—affecting 1 to 1.5 percent of the global population.

In 1941, early on in this area of research, prison psychologist Hervey Cleckley published the bestseller *The Mask of Sanity*, noting sixteen behavioural traits that formed a specific profile for the violent career criminals he interacted with on a daily basis. It was Cleckley's research that later inspired Dr Robert Hare, a Canadian prison psychologist from British Columbia, to develop the Hare Psychopathy Checklist, used today throughout the world for identifying the specific condition. The checklist consists of twenty questions designed to measure the degree of psychopathy in individuals. The higher the score, the more serious the condition. With 40 the highest score, and 0 the lowest, Hare considered a score of 30 or more the clinical definition for the dangerous psychopath. He debuted his work in the 1970s, and it was revised in the 1990s. The Hare Psychopathy Checklist-Revised (HRC-R) is today accepted by those in criminal psychology as the best method to determine the presence and level of psychopathy in a given person. The procedure now consists of an interview and a review of history, all done in a controlled setting by a clinician. Hare's Checklist helps doctors assess the degree of danger an individual poses based on their score and is today widely used by law enforcement communities for assessment purposes.

Psychopathy does not manifest itself suddenly. Much research has been expended on the neurobiology of violence that shows a strong genetic component. Recent studies of psychopaths using MRI and PET scan technology to map brain activity have definitively answered a very old, important argument: Are psychopaths born, or made? Nature or nurture? Neurobiological studies of psychopaths shows they are indeed a product of nature. The violent psychopath's brain imagery shows reduced connections between the amygdala, the brain's control centre for processing fear and rage, and the frontal lobe that determines how fear and rage are processed, and where feelings such as empathy and guilt originate. This connectivity between the two regions of the brain is wired differently in the psychopathic brain. This is not to say that upbringing or formative childhood experiences play no role, but the psychopathic personality begins in the brain.

Psychopaths are also fearless, a factor in their ability to repeatedly commit risky, high-profile crimes endangering their own lives as well as their victims'. Although the vast majority of psychopaths do not commit serious crimes, their personalities are very often destructive to those closely associated with them. They can suck the life out of their closest friends, families, and lovers, becoming quickly bored before moving on to new love conquests and friends to manipulate for their own self-interest. This is not to suggest that your lying, cheating old boyfriend or two-timing, self-centred ex-girlfriend is afflicted, yet, with the criminal and violent psychopath, no one is safe. Psychologist and neuroscientist Abigail Marsh described to *National Geographic* in 2018 how her study of children with psychopathic tendencies found that their amygdalas were smaller and that they showed a reduced response to frightening images.

Further, "anger is central to psychopathic violence," and is often triggered over the most trivial issues most people would shrug off as an unpleasant encounter. Psychopaths protect their fragile self-esteem at all costs, seeking sanctuary in a high degree of narcissism. The danger lies in the lack of reason and empathy; the psychopath's response is mitigated by their own desires and lack of concern for others—not empathy or reason. The lack of rationale or reason—a trait that defines us as human—is what makes the brain of a psychopath truly incorrigible.

These are medical understandings and legal nuances that cops, lawyers, judges, and juries were not aware of in 1966, as several high-profile psychopaths stalked their prey that fateful summer.

***

The first spree or rampage killer of note to garner public interest, prior to 1966, was Charles Starkweather, in 1958. Starkweather was nineteen, and his accomplice and lover, Carol Ann Fugate, was fourteen. They lived in Lincoln, Nebraska. Starkweather was bow-legged as a child and had a learning disability, leading him to be constantly teased and bullied. In high school, Starkweather adopted the persona of teen film star James Dean, immortalized in his youth rebellion film, *Rebel Without a Cause*. Starkweather had developed into a somewhat handsome lad, looked a bit like his film hero, and worked hard to emulate the film character's devil-may-care spirit. In December 1957, he robbed and killed a Lincoln gas station attendant who had earlier refused Starkweather credit to purchase a toy for Carol Ann. Starkweather drove the attendant to a side road and blew his head off with a shotgun. He was not suspected in the crime. On January 10, 1958, after dating Fugate for a year, Starkweather told Fugate's parents he wished to marry their daughter. An argument ensued, culminating with Starkweather taking a rifle from his car and shooting dead Fugate's parents and her baby sister. Starkweather and Fugate lived like a married couple for a week in Fugate's house while her family's bodies were stuffed in the outhouse.

Starkweather and Fugate were living in a madness shared by two, a juvenile couple killer with one dominant and one submissive personality who created their own reality where murder becomes an acceptable fact in their continually evolving ersatz world. The two lovers eventually left Fugate's house to avoid inquisitive family members and began a murder rampage that claimed seven more victims in and around the city of Lincoln, including one murder in eastern Wyoming, before returning to Lincoln to continue the carnage. There, the two teens terrorized, then murdered, the politically connected Ward family and their maid in the upper-class neighbourhood where Starkweather had once collected garbage. With brutal homicides now claiming Lincoln's social elites, the state governor ordered the Nebraska National Guard to patrol Lincoln's streets in armoured cars; every soldier in full battle gear. After a brief high-speed chase, Starkweather and Fugate eventually surrendered on January 29, 1958. When asked by police how he felt about his senseless three-week killing spree, Charlie replied, "It was fun."

Starkweather was executed the following year and Fugate would serve seventeen years in prison before being paroled in 1976. On January 30, 1958, with Starkweather and Fugate in custody, their killing rampage over, the *New York Times* reported the killing spree with just four paragraphs in the middle of page 41, headlined NEBRASKA TO TRY YOUTH AS SLAYER. The national print and television media basically ignored the story, leaving the details to regional news coverage in accordance with network news policy. The Starkweather rampage murders, then generally unknown outside the American Midwest, later inspired Hollywood films and television dramas such as *Badlands* (1973), *Kalifornia* (1993), and *Natural Born Killers* (1994). The first mass murderer(s) to terrorize and intrigue the public on a continental scale appeared in 1962, three years after spree killer Charles Starkweather was electrocuted.

The "Boston Strangler" was the first American serial killer to receive sustained international media attention. No case better demonstrates police shortcomings, cynical political intrigue, an exploitative media, and a misinformed public than this first, highly publicized "serial killer" of the early 1960s. He was the most feared killer in America—and Canada—during the period from 1962 to 1964, leaving fourteen unsolved murders in his wake. It was the first time that mass media played a major role in the story, making the Boston Strangler a key topic for family, social gatherings, and water-cooler work conversations. Listening to a radio program on the Boston Strangler from beneath the kitchen table or the next room, young children overheard their parents quietly discussing this modern-day Jack the Ripper. The Boston Strangler personified the boogeyman for many young Canadian children as well; they were vaguely aware Boston was somewhere far away, yet terrified by the salacious details overheard from adult conversations. When the fathers left the room, mothers would exchange excited whispers describing the most explicit details of the baffling, brutal homicides, inadvertently scaring children old enough to understand the tremendous violence visited upon these unsuspecting women.

Beginning in June 1962, eight elderly women would be viciously assaulted and murdered in the Boston area, their heads smashed in, sexually assaulted, strangled, their genitalia penetrated by household objects, and bodies left posed in demeaning positions for shock value awaiting those who found the victims. There was no sign of forced entry in any of the attacks, indicating the killer knew his victims or talked his way into these women's homes. Police obtained plenty of forensic evidence from the crime scenes, including substantial DNA evidence—its existence still unknown at the time. The Boston media, from the first murders in 1962, initially named the killer the "Silk Stocking Strangler" for his signature bow-tie calling card, a piece of the victim's clothing left wrapped around her neck in the shape of a large bow. With each new body, the media headlines became more hysterical and bordered on outright fear-mongering. These types of crimes could be expected in New York or Chicago, but in puritanical Boston?

Boston was a city in lockdown. Most women carried knives in their purses for protection and within six months of the first victim found, the local dog pounds and kennels had been emptied as women ventured outside Boston to purchase dogs they believed made them safer from possible attack.

The murders had come hard and fast, often within days of each other. A three-month period in the fall of 1962 went by without further Strangler attacks until December 1962, when twenty-year-old Sophie Clark, a university student, was found raped and murdered, yet her body was not posed post-mortem like other victims had been. Clark would be the first of more young female homicides attributed to the Strangler. Clark was young, and more notably, Black—meaning the killer was crossing racial lines, an unanticipated move. The print media made it clear no woman was safe. The public now viewed the Strangler as a larger-than-life predator who attacked young and old, White and Black. The Boston Police, however, were baffled. Were they dealing with multiple killers, or one? Many investigators believed there were other strong suspects for some of the crimes attributed to the Strangler, even preparing indictments against others for some of the killings attributed to the Strangler. It is a salient point, indicating police agencies in the early 1960s looked for patterns, but lacked the insight or knowledge criminal profiling would later add to the detective's tool kit.

The alleged Strangler would claim four more victims—all young women—throughout 1963. With at least one serial killer terrorizing the Boston area, medical examiners handed out autopsy reports of Strangler victims to anyone claiming to be from the press, a policy that would never happen today. Autopsies indicate the women were believed to have been attacked during the day, a fact the Boston media quickly exploited, printing the most scandalous details from the autopsy reports and instilling a siege mentality among the women of Boston. These coroner reports state what the victims were wearing, what they had last eaten, when and how they had died, and specific details as to how the murders were likely carried out.

In early January 1964, the Strangler struck for the last time. Nineteen-year-old Mary Sullivan was found strangled and violently raped. The state of Massachusetts now formed a statewide inter-agency task force to find the Boston Strangler. The governor and other state politicians took over the investigation, placing their future electability on the line. The failure to coordinate between law enforcement, Massachusetts politicians, and a relentless media only added to the chaos of the Boston Strangler case.

Known con man Albert DeSalvo made a jailhouse confession in 1965 after his arrest for other sexual assault and robbery charges. DeSalvo was just the man that the Boston establishment needed—an answer to the terror that had stalked their city—and he was quickly identified as the wanted man. He was not, however, actually charged with the crimes, and was later murdered under suspicious circumstances in prison in 1973. With our modern understanding of criminal profiling and DNA technology, controversy has swirled around the DeSalvo confession for over fifty years. In 2013, Boston Police positively identified DNA from seminal fluid samples from Mary Sullivan as Albert DeSalvo's— the only major breakthrough in this cold case. Did DeSalvo commit all of the crimes attributed to the Strangler? We may never know.

The Boston Strangler was the first case to be tried in the court of public opinion, fuelled by a modern media and meddled in by an anxious political elite. Boston had a conservative police force in one of America's oldest, most religious, and wealthiest cities, and their investigation was hampered by primitive forensic tools and a lack of understanding of the type of killer they were seeking. As soon as a plausible suspect was found, the case was for all intents and purposes solved, quietly closing the books on thirteen unsolved Boston sexual homicides.

The Boston Strangler was North America's elusive, sexually motivated mass killer, courtesy of the mass media. He was a terror that people and police departments assumed was an anomaly. Unbeknownst to Canadians at the time, London, Ontario—a nearby city whose population in 1966 was slightly smaller than Windsor's—was undergoing a rash of sexually motivated homicides by multiple killers in the mid-1960s, a catalogue of sexual homicide best told by author Michael Arntfield in *Murder City: The Untold Story of Canada's Serial Killer Capital, 1959–1984*. The Canadian public, outside of London, knew nothing of these homicides until Arntfield's book release in 2015. In 1965, even many London residents knew little of the predators who walked among them. The media never told us.

When, on the sweltering summer evening of June 25, 1966, eighteen-year-old Matthew Charles Lamb of Windsor, Ontario— an ex-convict released just seventeen days earlier from Kingston Penitentiary—stole a double-barrelled shotgun and ammunition from his uncle's residence on Ford Boulevard, then walked down this quiet residential street and fired shotgun shells into four strangers, it received wide regional media coverage. Windsor, Ontario, found itself confronted with its first "shooting spree" killer. And yet, the summer of mass murder and spree killings was only beginning.

A five-hour drive due south of Windsor sits the city of Chicago, Illinois, and the site of a horrific mass murder committed just three weeks after Lamb's killing spree. Richard Benjamin Speck was an unemployed twenty-five-year-old alcoholic drifter who, on July 13, 1966, raped a fifty-three-year-old woman at knifepoint—stealing her loaded handgun in the process. Later that same day, he sought employment at the Maritime Union Hall on Chicago's South Side. One hundred metres from the Union Hall was a townhouse that was housing student nurses. Speck had noticed a young woman enter the residence.

Later that same evening, July 13, Speck returned to the dormitory. Twenty-three-year-old nursing student Corazon Amurao responded to his knock on the front door. Speck pushed her back inside as he forced his way into the flat. He bound and gagged the women residents as they individually returned home throughout the early evening. With nine women helplessly restrained, Speck proceeded—one by one—to methodically torture, sexually assault, and murder eight young women throughout the course of the evening in one horrific act of depravity. Amurao, the young woman who first confronted Speck at the front door earlier that evening, was the sole survivor. She was able to roll herself across the floor and out of sight—unnoticed by the intoxicated Speck—spending a terrified night cringing under her bed, watching as Speck individually raped, stabbed, and strangled her roommates. Speck later admitted to "losing count" of his victims. The mass murderer was apprehended days later, found recovering in a local hospital from a botched suicide attempt from one slashed wrist. The American media loudly proclaimed this THE CRIME OF THE CENTURY, and for many, it marked the end of an age of innocence. Allowing for hyperbole and dissenting opinions among crime historians, Speck's killing spree remains etched in the annals of American crime as the first mass murder of the 20th century. Speck would spend the rest of his life in prison, passing away in 1991.

Richard Speck's horrific crime and subsequent global media attention was, like Matthew Lamb's before him, quickly surpassed by the spree shootings of Charles Joseph Whitman. In the early-morning hours of August 1, 1966—just two weeks after Speck shocked America and five weeks after Lamb shocked southern Ontario—Whitman stabbed his young wife and his mother to death while they slept, drove to the University of Texas at Austin, and climbed twenty-eight stories to the top of the Bell Tower, the tallest structure in the area. With a commanding view of the university campus and retail businesses aligned along its periphery, Whitman removed a number of firearms, ammunition, a first-aid kit, and a gallon of water from a duffle bag, and over the next ninety minutes, shot forty-five people—killing a total of sixteen, including his wife and mother. His killing spree was only ended when Whitman was shot dead at the scene by an Austin police officer.

An excellent student, an Eagle Scout, a decorated Marine with "sharpshooter" credentials, handsome, and physically fit, Whitman was awarded a university scholarship from the American military to study engineering at the University of Texas. Like Lamb, Whitman was obsessed with firearms; he was also proficient in their use and owned a virtual arsenal of weapons. Yet the twisted impulse to commit mass murder had been nurtured in Whitman's fantasies years before he acted out. Whitman had told a psychiatrist, well before he acted out his fantasy, of his growing compulsion to ascend the Bell Tower at the University of Texas and shoot people. His fears were dismissed by his psychiatrist, although the doctor did note Whitman was "filled with hostility." Whitman kept a personal daily journal recording his despair and helplessness at resisting his murderous fantasies. In the final months before acting out, Whitman appears to have developed hypergraphia, a compulsive need to record data and details outlining his thoughts and plans, a condition common to people with neurological problems. Whitman habitually wrote reminder notes to help him avoid negative behaviours, scolding himself, "Do not yell at your wife; Do not hit your wife." He insisted to his doctor and psychiatrist that there was something physically wrong with him, even leaving a suicide note before embarking on his mass murders requesting his brain be analyzed for irregularities following his death.

The autopsy of Whitman's brain indeed showed an undiagnosed brain tumour that may well have contributed to his violent compulsions that overwhelmed him in the months leading up to his killing spree. Whitman's body count had, in 1966, made him the most prolific spree killer in American history, unsurpassed until 1984, when James Huberty, a middle-aged, married but disgruntled security guard, opened fire on patrons, killing twenty-one and wounding nineteen at a McDonald's restaurant in San Ysidro, California.

The Speck and Whitman killings both occurred within a two-month period following Lamb's killing spree in Windsor, Ontario, marking the summer of 1966 as unique with three rare, high-profile cases of mass murder that stunned Canadians and Americans alike. Speck, like Whitman, claimed more victims than Lamb, and being Americans, both criminals garnered more media attention. These three killers were considered aberrations, human anomalies whose unfathomable crimes were too baffling to be understood by the general public and thus unlikely to be repeated. Rather, they were canaries in a coal mine; the calm before the storm; omens of the mass murderers that have today become all too common in contemporary Western culture. Homicide investigators soon found themselves on the cusp of an escalating paradigm shift—cold-blooded multiple murders for no clear motive—that they were ill-equipped to handle.

But on June 25, 1966, there was only Matthew Charles Lamb—a troubled youth, a deadly random crime, a terrified public, and an unprepared police force. No one knew what was to come, but it's not the beginning of the story. How did he get there?

CHAPTER FIVE
Matthew Charles Lamb

> Once he was a child, a beautiful child, a child of clay
> Shaped and molded into what he is today
> But who is to blame for this child of clay?
> —Jimmie F. Rodgers (1967)

MATTHEW CHARLES LAMB WAS BORN ON JANUARY 5, 1948, in Windsor, Ontario, the child of an unwed fifteen-year-old mother and an absent father. Lamb never knew his father, who met an unnatural death in the United States while Lamb was still a child. Abandoned by his mother as an infant, Lamb was shuffled around among his extended family or periodically placed in foster care. The closest Lamb ever came to a home was living with his maternal grandmother and her second husband at 2136 York Street in south-central Windsor. Details of Lamb's formative years are sketchy, but we know Lamb's mother made rare, short visits every one to three years to see her son. Lamb never displayed any emotional attachment or interest in his mother, or any other adult, with the possible exception of his grandmother and a favourite uncle. Lamb metaphorically expressed his indifference toward people as "everyone else appearing as bugs to him."

Born into the lower working class, Lamb's childhood was dysfunctional but certainly not unique. Lamb's early social interaction with other people was distinguished by shyness, apathy, and random violent outbursts. Lamb had few friends growing up, preferring to be alone, but he did have one close childhood friend, Gregory Sweet, with whom Lamb maintained a lifelong friendship. Sweet claimed Lamb's violent streak and sadistic tendencies became apparent at an early age. Lamb habitually terrified his younger cousins by locking them in his bedroom closet and threatening them with horrifying punishments. He once beat a younger male cousin so badly the boy was hospitalized for his injuries. These incidents expressed the inner rage that grew exponentially as Lamb entered his teenage years.

Lamb would later tell his defence attorney how his step-grandfather, Christopher Collins, subjected both Lamb and his maternal grandmother to physical and emotional abuse. Lamb particularly resented Collins for constantly referring to him as "the little bastard," a demeaning insult for any child born out of wedlock during this era of rigid social mores. The predominant middle-class values imposed by elites on the working class prior to the late 1960s were an effective tool of social control. Unwed mothers and single-parent families were stigmatized as social and moral failings. As an eight-year-old boy attending elementary school in 1963, I experienced first-hand the consequences of falling outside the powerful conformity of our then prevailing social attitudes. My parents had separated for a short period and, fifty years later, I can clearly recall the smirking faces and taunts of my male classmates, whispering "Hey! Fatherless!" whenever I walked past their desks. In vain, I looked to my homeroom teacher for support. Only once did she come to my defence with a half-hearted vocal admonishment of, "That's enough, boys," before the taunts immediately resumed. Fortunately, my parents soon reconciled, but not before I punched the main instigator of my torment one day after school, effectively ending any further insults from my classmates.

Following Lamb's arrest for his 1966 killing spree, Detective Sergeant Jim Ure interviewed Greg Sweet, Lamb's closest friend, for background information on Lamb. Sweet made a poor impression on Ure: "Yeah, I remember that Sweet guy, a pimply-faced kid who didn't impress me at all." The fact Sweet was present during many of Lamb's early antisocial and sadistic acts did not endear him to Ure. Sweet told the officer, and later the media, how Lamb was just seven years old when he held a knife to the throat of a younger boy until the boy ate dog feces. When Ure asked why Sweet did not intervene during this specific incident, Sweet said he "was afraid to interfere this one time." Sweet also told Ure how he and Lamb became fascinated with weapons by the age of twelve: "We always had guns and learned how to use them." When he and Lamb were about thirteen years old, Lamb loaded his shotgun one evening and, in a prophetic act, calmly walked down a quiet residential street firing directly at the homes of people he (Lamb) didn't like. Police were not notified so nothing came of it. Lamb also inscribed the names of police officers he disliked on the shell casings of live ammunition for his weapon collection, indicative of his early hatred for authority figures, especially the police. These chilling but prescient examples of Lamb's acting out his violent impulses—especially the careless discharging of firearms in public places—were signatures present in Lamb's later crimes, culminating with his murder rampage at eighteen years of age.

Lamb also liked making homemade bombs shaped as weapons. On one occasion, a bomb he fashioned from an old .50-calibre shell casing accidentally exploded, spraying Lamb's leg with shrapnel. Police were again not notified. Young boys everywhere during the 1960s made homemade explosives as a form of amusement, building makeshift rockets inspired more by the media hype of the space age and the riveting "race to the moon" media war between the Soviet Union and the USA. Everyone knew mixing saltpetre, sulphur, and barbecue charcoal (carbon) in specific proportions produced explosive powder.

Saltpetre and sulphur could be purchased, without a prescription, in two-kilogram bags from a local pharmacy in those days, while barbecue charcoal was readily available. Boys typically used toilet paper rolls or discarded tin cans packed with homemade explosive to construct and launch their rudimentary rockets—but not to design weapons as Lamb liked to do.

Lamb joined the Windsor Sea Cadets like many local boys, but he didn't last long. His personality was antithetical to the demands of mandatory conformity, structured discipline, and obeying of orders demanded by the military. He also tried joining the Ku Klux Klan, according to Greg Sweet, but could not find a local chapter in Windsor. Lamb apparently had no particular dislike for people of African descent, but did hold racist views that were common among many in Windsor, who linked their neighbouring border city's high crime rates with its large Black population. Revealingly, Ure recalls Sweet telling him Lamb was a "switch hitter," a slang term for bisexuality. There is no evidence Lamb's sexual preference was in any way linked to his violent behaviour, but his sexual orientation would have contributed to his self-isolation, as homosexual acts were still a criminal offence in 1966 and socially unacceptable.

Lamb attended a number of local schools due to his frequent changes of address, residing with various family members. He received good school grades—attributable to his above-average IQ—yet demonstrated a restlessness and inability to concentrate or focus for any length of time on schoolwork. Lamb was habitually shy and standoffish with fellow classmates and didn't like to partake in group activities. He preferred to be alone and always declined social invitations with excuses such as "I don't like to dance," an attitude Lamb maintained throughout his academic years. By 1963, Lamb began carrying a knife to school and showed it off at every opportunity, enjoying the negative attention he received, until he was suspended from Assumption Catholic Secondary School. Lamb dropped out of school for good shortly thereafter, having failed to complete grade ten.

Another student attending Assumption Secondary with Lamb, although two grades ahead, was performing much better academically, and excelled in Assumption's sports teams. Andrew Woloch was a grade-twelve student busily preparing for graduation—excited about his future and proud to be the first in his family to pursue a university education. Woloch would likely have paid little attention to the likes of Lamb as they passed each other daily in the school's chatty and crowded hallways. Shortly after leaving school, Lamb worked various jobs but never lasted much longer than a month before quitting or being fired for inability to take direction from superiors.

***

In order to understand Lamb's path to murder, it is necessary to reconstruct his activities and the sequence of events from February 1964 until his killing spree in June 1966. This critical period of escalating criminality has gone unexplored. Lamb had just turned sixteen years old when, on February 10, 1964, he acted on his pathological hatred for police with an unprovoked physical assault on an officer. Constable Donald Graham of the Village of Riverside Police Department was moonlighting to supplement his modest police salary, working security at a teenage Valentine's Day dance held at the Riverside Arena, then a popular sports venue and meeting place for Riverside teenagers. Graham was standing outside the arena's front doors chatting with a fellow officer as teenagers began leaving the arena after the dance when Lamb suddenly jumped on the officer's back and began punching him in the face. Graham, a tall and muscular officer, quickly subdued his physically smaller attacker. Lamb could have seriously wounded or perhaps killed the police officer, had he so chosen, as a physical search found Lamb was carrying a knife, a pair of brass knuckles, and a heavy bicycle chain inside his jacket at the time of the assault. There was no apparent motive for the attack, aside perhaps from Lamb's inner rage unleashed to bolster his reputation as a local badass before the large crowd of astonished teenagers.

Lamb was subsequently convicted for assault under the Juvenile Delinquents Act and was sentenced to six months incarceration at the House of Concord, a juvenile facility operated by the Salvation Army, which stressed Christian principles and ethical teachings for wayward boys. It was the first time Lamb had come to the attention of the police and courts. His six months of rehabilitation were marked by total indifference and lack of interest in making any positive behavioural changes.

Released from the juvenile facility in July 1964, Lamb returned to Windsor and moved in with an uncle for a short period before being asked to leave. He may have found temporary lodging at the home of his only friend, Greg Sweet, who resided with his mother on Jarvis Avenue in the Village of Riverside. Lamb had previously lived with the Sweet family for a short period in 1962, although Sweet's mother was not fond of her son's close relationship with Lamb, once remarking to her son that Lamb was in dire need of psychiatric help. During the late summer and fall of 1964, Lamb bounced around Riverside finding shelter wherever and whenever it was offered.

The critical months preceding Lamb's next violent confrontation with police in the dying days of 1964 are instructive. His actions reveal an impulsive and chameleon-like personality with an enduring fascination with guns. Lamb repeatedly and openly bragged of his desire to kill police officers—a fantasy he had cultivated from the age of twelve. Roger Hammond (a pseudonym), today a veteran of the Royal Canadian Mounted Police, had known Lamb for most of his life. Discussing his childhood relationship with Lamb, Hammond began by stating: "I am convinced that if Matthew Lamb had never become close friends with Greg Sweet, he never would have shot all those people back in 1966." Hammond's opinion regarding Sweet is unsubstantiated conjecture and must be viewed as such, although Hammond's personal relationship with Lamb and detailed knowledge of the events of late 1964 provides insight into the character of a killer in the making.

Hammond grew up in the town of Tecumseh, then a small village bordering the eastern boundary of Riverside. He lived in the house closest to Lakeview Marine, a boat and motor retail store that sold sporting gear, camping equipment, and guns, then located on Lesperance Road at Riverside Drive. In 1964, Lakeview Marine stood alone in an undeveloped area of open fields perpetually pounded by Michigan's southerly winds which blew in across the shallow waters of Lake St. Clair before emptying into the narrow strait of the Detroit River on its long eastern journey to the Atlantic Ocean. Bernie and Roy Desjardins, two brothers who built and operated Lakeview Marine, were hot-rod enthusiasts who built customized race cars on their store's property. "It was a pretty cool place to hang around when you were a kid," Hammond recalls, "with hot rods and motors all around. It naturally attracted every young boy in the area." The Desjardinses, in addition to being "cool" role models for the local boys, possessed a strong social conscience, acting as surrogate fathers to some of the young boys who appeared "rough around the edges." The brothers let these boys earn a little pocket money by performing small jobs around Lakeview Marine, such as fetching items from the stockroom or sweeping the floors. The Desjardins tried to instill in these boys a sense of responsibility and an appreciation for earning their money honestly.

In the autumn of 1964, Lamb was one of those kids who hung around Lakeview Marine. "The Desjardins brothers tried helping Lamb by giving him part-time work so he could earn a couple of honest bucks," Hammond recalls. The other local boys all knew Lamb had had a pretty rough childhood but accepted the charming drifter nevertheless. Hammond was a conscientious boy from a good family who took a real liking to Lamb, and by the fall of 1964, the two had become friends. Hammond remembers Greg Sweet as something of an outsider who appeared to avoid Lakeview Marine: "Sweet was perceived to be a rough kid parents told their sons to avoid. He was generally viewed as sullen and confrontational by the other teenagers who hung around Lakeview Marine." In fairness to Sweet, he was afflicted from a young age with facial scars caused by a severe case of teenage acne—a common problem for adolescent boys of the 1960s when effective medications were not yet available—which likely contributed to Sweet's acerbic attitude. Hammond remembers how Sweet was constantly teased by school classmates: "Sweet was not a particularly big kid and was often beaten up by school bullies whenever he bravely tried to stand up for himself." Sweet, like Lamb, grew up facing a host of challenges to overcome, more so than the other boys congregating around Lakeview Marine in the warm autumn days of 1964.[2]

"Lamb was notably shy around a large group of people, but in a one-on-one conversation was exceptionally charming and likeable and could talk the pants off a stranger," Hammond laughingly recalls. "Lamb's charm and quick wit made him a fun guy to be around. He was a handsome guy," Hammond adds, although he doesn't recall Lamb ever dating or expressing interest in the young women who sought his attentions. Hammond saw nothing unusual in this, and was genuinely surprised upon learning of Lamb's suspected bisexuality. He was, however, aware of Lamb's violent nature, and when personally threatened by it, felt compelled to end their friendship.

During the fall weather, local boys traditionally hunted for pheasant in the fields around Lakeview Marine. If a boy could not afford his own weapon, the Desjardinses would lend the boy a shotgun to hunt with. Gun laws were not as strict in the 1960s as they are today. One crisp autumn morning, Lamb and Hammond went pheasant hunting together, both armed with shotguns. Lamb had borrowed his weapon from the Desjardinses. The two boys

---

2   Greg Sweet returned my call, but let it be known that he was not interested in commenting further on his relationship with Lamb or other boys during this period.

had shot a couple of pheasants and were walking through the scrub brush with Hammond leading the way when Lamb suddenly fired a shotgun round into the dirt directly between Hammond's legs. Visibly shaken, Hammond turned around and yelled: "What are you, crazy? You could have killed me! What was that all about"? Lamb responded with his quirky, sinister giggle that Hammond always found unsettling and alien to Lamb's otherwise easygoing nature. "I could have killed you," Lamb said, his shotgun pointed directly at Hammond's chest. Although frightened, Hammond pretended to laugh the episode off to defuse the situation. Making up an excuse to end their hunting excursion, Hammond later told the Desjardins brothers about the incident and Lamb was thereafter denied the privilege of borrowing weapons from Lakeview Marine. "Lamb seldom came around Lakeview Marine after his gun-borrowing rights had been revoked. Hunting season was over anyway." The weather was growing colder and the local ring-necked pheasants, with their distinctive white feather collars and gold plumage, either hunkered down in the local scrub brush to ride out the winter or headed south for warmer climes. Residents of Riverside and Tecumseh also recognized the periodic cold sting riding on the winds blowing off Lake St. Clair as the first signs of winter.

Around 6 p.m. on Christmas Eve 1964, the Desjardinses, in their traditional holiday gesture, lit the store's interior wood stove to kick off the popular Christmas party they threw every year for the local boys who worked part-time at Lakeview Marine. They extended the guest list to include those boys who regularly hung around their store. Hammond remembers that particular night in detail: "The Desjardins brothers gave us boys a beer or two each just to let us feel like grown men, but certainly not enough for us to get drunk. We sat around the fire drinking and telling dirty jokes or played scrum hockey on the outdoor skating rink." Every winter the Desjardinses built an ice rink equipped with artificial lighting for night hockey games played in the empty fields behind Lakeview Marine.

Lamb was visibly intoxicated when he first arrived at the Christmas party, yet spent most of the night playing scrum hockey without incident. When the celebrations ended, Bernie Desjardins locked the doors to Lakeview Marine and turned off the exterior lights to the skating rink. The store and its rustic surroundings were plunged back into darkness as all the boys— except one—set off for their warm homes and waiting families on the most festive night of the Christian calendar. Bernie Desjardins offered to drive Hammond to his aunt's home, with whom Hammond was temporarily residing. Desjardins had been dating Hammond's aunt for some time and had made arrangements to spend Christmas Eve with his girlfriend.

While driving away from Lakeview Marine, Hammond and Desjardins noticed Lamb sitting on a snowbank, alone in the dark, his coat collar turned up to block the cold winds. Hammond mentioned how lonely and rejected Lamb must be feeling, apparently having nowhere to go on Christmas Eve. He had heard a rumour that Lamb had no home since being asked to leave his uncle's residence some weeks earlier. Desjardins briefly considered going back to get Lamb, believing no one should be alone on Christmas Eve. On any other night he would have done so, but this particular Christmas Eve was special. Desjardins had spent the past few months preparing his big surprise for Hammond's aunt on this very night. He could not risk an intoxicated Lamb possibly ruining the most important night of his life. Inside his winter coat pocket, Desjardins carried a small red box with a gold bow containing a diamond engagement ring. He was nervous but determined to propose marriage that night.

A light snow had begun to fall as Desjardins's car pulled into his girlfriend's driveway. Shaking off the cold and settling on the couch in the living room, Desjardins was about to pop the big question when the telephone rang. The call was for him. It was the Ontario Provincial Police calling to inform him of a reported break-in at Lakeview Marine, requesting he accompany an officer back to the store to determine what items, if any, were missing.

Desjardins was frustrated, telling the police dispatcher he had just locked up his store less than thirty minutes ago and was sure there must be some mistake. The OPP nevertheless insisted and, together, Desjardins and Constable Cail Miller drove the short distance back to the store.

Random snow squalls began blowing off the lake, reducing visibility on Riverside Drive. Miller turned on the police cruiser's emergency lights as a precaution to oncoming traffic before turning left into the parking lot of Lakeview Marine. The smashed front display window confirmed there had indeed been a break-in. A cursory inspection inside the store confirmed a number of firearms and ammunition boxes were missing from the display cases, although everything else appeared untouched.

Walking around to the rear of the store, Miller noticed a fresh set of footprints in the slush—the field had been soaked by two days of rain before the weather turned cold—leading directly across the back field toward a gully obscured by wild brush, difficult to see in the darkness, approximately thirty metres from the rear of the store. The two men were approaching the dense underbrush when Desjardins suddenly stopped walking. He intuitively sensed danger and, using the excuse of poor visibility, convinced Constable Miller to abandon the search until morning, when the tracks would be easier to follow in the daylight. Miller reasoned the suspect would be long gone from the crime scene anyway, so the two men turned around and had begun walking back toward the police car when gunfire suddenly erupted from the gully, two bullets just missing Miller and Desjardins. Both men dove face first into the muddy field and rolled into a furrow for protection. Miller— noting the direction of fire from the muzzle flashes—immediately returned fire with his .38-calibre service revolver. A voice suddenly called out from the darkness: "Don't shoot! I give up. I'm coming out." The figure of a man with hands held above his head slowly materialized out of the darkness. As the assailant got closer, a shocked Bernie Desjardins watched as Constable Miller threw Lamb against the police car, handcuffed him, searched him for weapons, and put him in the back seat of the police cruiser. Before leaving, Lamb gave up the location of the stolen weapons and ammunition.

Lamb sat quietly as they drove to the police station, saying nothing and purposely avoiding having to look Desjardins and Miller in the eye. Christians love to tell their young children that a Christmas snow is a "magic snow" promising good fortune. The merits of that myth shone on Desjardins and Miller that night, as Lamb was a competent, self-taught marksman whose shots rarely missed at such close distance. Desjardins had felt the air pressure from a bullet whizzing past his ear, fired from Lamb's improvised ambush site.

Both men were angry and perplexed. Lamb had enjoyed Desjardins's holiday hospitality less than an hour earlier, and now showed his appreciation by robbing Lakeview Marine and almost killing Desjardins. Constable Miller was enraged at his suspect for trying to shoot him in the back as he walked toward his police car having already abandoned the search for a suspect until daylight. Miller wondered why Lamb hadn't left the crime scene immediately after stealing the guns. Why would someone sit in a ditch in the bitter winter cold on Christmas Eve, knowing police would soon arrive to investigate the robbery, rather than make an easy getaway? Moreover, why did Lamb open fire only after Miller and Desjardins retreated from Lamb's position? Had Lamb just waited until Miller and Desjardins drove away, he could have fled the crime scene undetected. Hammond answers these questions without hesitation:

> It was no big secret Lamb had been hiding in the gully with the stolen guns just waiting for a cop to show up at Lakeview Marine to investigate the break-in. Lamb always bragged to me and other guys from the east side how he would kill a cop one day. We had no cause to disbelieve him. I don't think he [Lamb] expected Bernie [Desjardins] to show up when the cops came,

but everybody knew Lamb had prepared an ambush that night, just waiting for the cops to respond to the break-in. Lamb bragged about it! That's what I remember anyway.

The evidence supports Hammond's account. The similarities in Lamb's modus operandi for his 1964 and 1966 shooting incidents are striking. His improvised ambush to await police arriving at Lakeview Marine on December 24, 1964, was a tactic repeated less than two years later on June 25, 1966, when Lamb lay in wait for police from an improvised sniper's nest in the backyard of Anne Heaton's home. When questioned by police two days after his Ford Boulevard shooting spree as to why he left a pile of shotgun ammunition in the field behind the Heaton home, Lamb admitted as much, stating, "Yeah, I did the same thing the last time."

For stealing three handguns, a double-barrelled shotgun, ammunition, and shooting at Constable Miller and Bernie Desjardins, Lamb was convicted of breaking and entering, theft, and discharging a firearm dangerous to the public peace. The presiding judge at Lamb's 1965 trial, J. Arthur Hanrahan, received a pre-sentencing report describing Lamb as a juvenile offender with a prior conviction for attacking Constable Don Graham outside Riverside Arena earlier that same year, an offense for which Lamb served six months in a juvenile facility. The *Windsor Star* quoted Judge Hanrahan's ruling, "Burglars we always have with us," he said. "Fortunately, those willing to shoot at another human being [...] are in the minority. When it occurs, however, it is conduct meriting a penitentiary sentence." Justice Saul Nosanchuk—Lamb's future defence attorney—believes that Judge Hanrahan concluded there was no hope of rehabilitation for Lamb, sentencing the sixteen-year-old to two years at Kingston Penitentiary, the minimum sentence required for incarceration in a Canadian federal penitentiary. Lamb was convicted for his Lakeview Marine robbery at a time when juvenile offenders charged with serious crimes could be tried as adults and sentenced accordingly.

Fifty years on, Hammond remains convinced, just like Greg Sweet's mother, that had Lamb received psychological intervention earlier in life he would have taken a different path: "Lamb was 'a nice guy' who would never have committed those shootings had he had a better home life and not befriended some unsavoury characters. I am absolutely sure of that. To be totally honest about Matthew Lamb, I really liked the guy!"

***

Psychological examinations are mandatory for all incoming inmates at Kingston Penitentiary. After Lamb arrived in April 1965, prison doctors assessed him as a very aggressive and immature young man fascinated with guns, obsessed with violent fantasies, and having little self-control or self-discipline. Lamb's stay at Kingston Penitentiary was not without incident. He once got into a fight with another inmate and spent an extended period in solitary confinement. Returned to the general population, a night guard found Lamb kneeling on the floor beside his bed one evening, pushing a broom handle up his rectum. This incident led to an immediate appointment with Dr George Scott, Director of Psychiatry at Kingston Penitentiary. Lamb's nightly activity set off alarm bells. For a young man with homosexual preferences, had this incident occurred today as opposed to in 1966, it would not likely be considered a psychological emergency. Rather, it would suggest Lamb was masturbating in a manner that gave him sexual satisfaction. Had he been a heterosexual prisoner caught masturbating in his cell, it wouldn't even warrant a notation in the night guard's end-of-shift report. But psychiatry in the 1960s treated homosexuality as a mental illness, and Canadian law codified homosexuality, or sodomy, as a punishable criminal offence.

Dr Scott placed Lamb under sedation and stated in his report: "I think this young man is developing a mental illness of a 'hypomanic' [a mania of low intensity] nature." Scott requested a further psychological assessment that concluded Lamb harboured violent fantasies of fights, robberies, and shootings. In a similar incident, Lamb was on janitorial duty when observed walking down the prison corridor with a mop handle shoved up his rectum, laughing as he dragged the mop behind him. Lamb shrugged off the incident, telling Scott he did it "as a joke to aggravate the guard on duty in [my] cellblock." Unconvinced, Scott admitted Lamb to Kingston Psychiatric Hospital for treatment of possible mental illness and possible "hypomania" on March 18, 1966, just three months before Lamb's outright release from prison. Scott wrote in his report that he wasn't sure if Lamb was experiencing a mental breakdown or was just "putting on an act." Prisoners often faked sickness, hoping to be referred to the prison hospital where clean bedsheets, better food, and no work assignment offered temporary respite from the monotony and discomfort of the cellblock.

One month later, Lamb was released from the psychiatric hospital and again returned to the general prison population. The prison hospital's final report assessed Lamb's prognosis as poor, specifying it was their opinion Lamb was a "recidivist risk likely to reoffend" following his release from prison. Dr Scott added an addendum to Lamb's final hospital psychiatric report, stating it was his belief Lamb "was in a marginal state of mental pathology…and that a schizoid element in his behaviour had developed." There were also signs of depression—Lamb bore scars on his wrist from a suicide attempt while incarcerated.

Despite his misgivings, Scott not only refused to send Lamb to Oak Ridge Facility for the Criminally Insane, but actually signed off on Lamb's early release from Kingston Penitentiary, with Lamb having served just fourteen months of his two-year prison sentence for the incident at Lakeview Marine only sixteen months before. Scott had the authority to either keep Lamb in the prison's psychiatric hospital or transfer him to Oak Ridge after Lamb's two-year prison sentence expired, yet chose neither option despite acknowledging he was "admittedly nervous" about releasing Lamb back into the community.

So why did Dr Scott agree to early release for Lamb, after he'd served barely half of his original two-year sentence, if he was as mentally unstable as Dr Scott believed? Why didn't Scott, at a minimum, insist Lamb undergo intensive psychiatric treatment while in Kingston Penitentiary's hospital until he completed his two-year sentence? Dr Scott would be provided an opportunity to explain these contradictions later at Lamb's capital murder trial for the brutal shotgun killings of two innocent Windsor youths and the wounding of two others, just days following Lamb's early prison release.

On June 9, 1966, Matthew Lamb walked out of Kingston Penitentiary a free man, carrying one suitcase and a one-way bus ticket to Windsor, Ontario. His uncle, Stanley Hasketh, had agreed to Lamb living at Hasketh's family home at 1912 Ford Boulevard on the condition that Lamb find employment and stay out of trouble. It would prove to be a fateful decision.

CHAPTER SIX:
Watching the Devil Dance

TWO DAYS AFTER BLASTING HIS WAY INTO
Canadian criminal history, Matthew Charles Lamb appeared
before Windsor's Magistrates Court with only the judge, court
stenographer, a single reporter from the *Windsor Star,* and arresting officer Detective Sergeant Jim Ure in attendance. Court proceedings were surreptitiously moved up an hour earlier than
scheduled to avoid a crowd of curious spectators and media
hounds ready to cover the sensational crime for their newspapers
or to pad television ratings. Everyone was anxious for a glimpse
of the young man who, two days earlier, gunned down four innocent strangers in a residential Windsor neighbourhood for no
apparent reason.

Lamb sat alone on the long wooden bench in the prisoner's dock, usually filled with detainees awaiting their turn to
shuffle up before the presiding judge to hear their charges read
and court dates set. Lamb's body language and loud audible

yawns articulated his indifference toward the court proceedings. Handcuffed and brought before the magistrate, Lamb was charged with the capital murder of Edith Chaykoski—a crime carrying a mandatory death sentence upon conviction. Capital punishment would not be abolished in Canada until 1976, a decade later. The magistrate ordered a standard pretrial psychiatric examination to determine Lamb's mental state.

Immediately following Lamb's first court appearance, Dr Walter Yaworsky, a Windsor psychiatrist, interviewed the defendant at the Windsor county jail for one hour. Lamb was not asked to fill out any psychiatric questionnaires or given the standard Rorschach test (the ink-blot cards) in use since 1921 or the Minnesota Multiphasic Personality Inventory (MMPI) used to assess personality traits and psychopathology. These were the most reliable diagnostic tools for determining underlying emotional trauma and psychotic thinking patterns available in the 1960s.

Lamb dominated his interview. Loudly proclaiming his innocence, Lamb told Yaworsky he had no memory of any shooting rampage, yet when informed of the death of Chaykoski, Lamb giggled and said, "Poor broad"—that same sadistic giggle his friend Roger Hammond had always found so disturbing. Purposely avoiding Yaworsky's specific questions about the night of the shootings, Lamb made a transparent attempt to impress the psychiatrist by proclaiming that "he would kill himself if he found out he had indeed committed the crime." He also had made claims that he had intended to commit suicide, by shooting himself, on the night of June 25. Of course, he then changed his mind and ventured outside—armed to the teeth—to gun down strangers.

Lamb frequently changed the subject while strutting around the county jail's holding room, complaining to Yaworsky how "he just wanted a normal life like other kids his age," then quickly changing tack by bragging of the money he'd saved for a new car, while cautioning the doctor that he had "the kinds of friends you don't mess with." Lamb displayed all the classic traits of the violent psychopath: the self-centred sense of entitlement, grandiosity, and attempts to establish control over the interview process. Lamb's one-hour interview with Yaworsky appeared to be, on the surface, a long rambling and incoherent rant, yet it contained a well-concealed logic designed to convince Yaworsky of Lamb's mental instability.

Yaworsky's diagnosis of Lamb, based entirely on this one-hour interview, described a young man suffering from a "hypomanic mood," evident by Lamb's agitation and frequent changing of the subject, and reported his "total amnesia" regarding the shootings. It was Yaworsky's opinion that Lamb suffered from "a condition causing a marked defect in his ability to feel or appreciate emotion-based behaviour with a subsequent inability to feel remorse, guilt, or shame." In other words, Lamb displayed the basic characteristics of the psychopathic personality. Yaworsky, of course, did not have the "Psychopathy Checklist" at his disposal, or even a sophisticated understanding of what a psychopath was, particularly in the criminal justice setting. Instead, the doctor made a diagnostic leap, declaring Lamb to be "insane...having suffered a temporary 'psychotic break' from reality causing 'complete amnesia' at the time of the killing." He continued, saying that the break made Lamb "incapable of appreciating the consequences of his actions" or able to participate in his own defence. Yaworsky offered no quantifiable evidence to support his assertion of insanity, other than citing (and believing) Lamb's claim of amnesia and his bizarre behaviour throughout the interview. The diagnosis was apparently based entirely on this one-hour jailhouse conversation, without the benefit of psychological testing to substantiate his conclusions.

Law enforcement officers have long been familiar with the psychopath's predictable antics and proven ability to con medical professionals. One of the psychopath's favourite interview games is "duping delight," in which he lies just to see if he can get away with it. The psychopath manipulates his listener by adopting a self-confident swagger and making sweeping, inconsistent statements. He uses these tactics to confuse the mental health assessor, making it difficult for the listener to properly follow the psychopath's self-reporting. The psychiatrist is led to believe that he or she is witnessing acute mental confusion, irrational and inconsistent behaviour associated with a lost sense of reality and a lack of understanding of consequences. Microexpressions, like an ill-timed smirk or slight grin—or even a giggle—are giveaways of duping delight. The psychopath's objective is fairly simple: to portray himself as incapable of appreciating the nature of the crimes he commits in order to minimize punishment.

Yaworsky's jailhouse interview with Lamb is a textbook example of duping delight—or what my former RCMP colleagues cynically named the "devil dance." As uniformed officers in the 1970s, we would sometimes listen in on interviews between violent, psychopathic offenders and local psychologists ordered by the courts to evaluate the offenders' mental stability. Both frustrating and amusing was observing the look of shock and fascination on the psychologist's face when confronted with an offender's unpredictable and outrageous behaviour—as they frantically scribbled observations in their notebooks, recording every nuance of abnormal behaviour listed in the psychiatric bible, then the DSM-1. In the 1960s and 1970s, most professional analysts lacked experience dealing with violent psychopaths and the post-arrest "madman"—an act so familiar to law enforcement. According to his few friends, Lamb learned the essentials of the devil dance at a much earlier age, mastering the manipulative verbal skills and hyper-physical displays of performance art at which the psychopath naturally excels.

Yaworsky stood up in front of a judge and declared that Lamb was mentally unfit to stand trial. Unconvinced by Yaworsky's psychiatric evaluation, the presiding magistrate ordered Lamb sent to St. Thomas Ontario Psychiatric Hospital for a more thorough psychiatric examination. On June 29, four days after the shootings, Lamb was examined by Dr James Dolan, the clinical director of psychiatry at the hospital in St. Thomas, Ontario.

Lamb did not perform the devil dance for Dr Dolan, probably assuming Dolan would quickly recognize the deception used to great effect on Dr Yaworsky two days earlier. In a complete reversal from his prior claim of "total amnesia" during the shootings told to Yaworsky, Lamb calmly gave Dolan a detailed account of his movements on the night of his shooting rampage. He admitted to arriving home from work in mid-afternoon and consuming approximately eight beers between 3 and 9 p.m. on Saturday, June 25. He had watched a violent television western before retiring to bed. Waking up just one hour later at 10 p.m., Lamb found and loaded his uncle's double-barrelled shotgun, telling Dolan his original intention was to "shoot himself." He failed to explain why he found it necessary to load both barrels of the shotgun and fill his pockets with ammunition in order to commit suicide. By placing himself as the original victim, Lamb was attempting to dismantle any whiff of premeditation. "Next thing I knew," he continued, "I was on the street." Dolan didn't press Lamb for an explanation, either failing to note its significance or dismissing the suicide claim for what it was—a deceptive ploy to obtain sympathy and raise doubts of "premeditation" and "intent" as factors in the murderous crime he would soon have to answer for.

Lamb told Dolan that as he began walking north down Ford Boulevard, he experienced symptoms correlating with a dissociative state—feeling as if he were watching "another person commit the crimes." He recalled shooting Edith Chaykoski shortly after "hearing a voice" tell her to "put up your hands." After shooting Chaykoski, Lamb fixated on "the terrified look on a young man's face [Woloch] before 'hearing another shot' and watching that man's body fall." Lamb recalled running across Ford Boulevard and seeing the silhouette of a girl standing inside a side screen door as he ran up her driveway, before "somehow shooting her." Lamb then fired a "potshot" at a passing car before "confronting an old lady [Anne Heaton] in a nearby house." It was "about this time he realized he was terribly confused" and began asking himself: "What am I doing here? Why am I holding a gun?" Lamb then lied to Dolan, claiming he left the woman's house and "tossed the gun away in a field" before flagging down a taxi at Pillette Road and Tecumseh Avenue for the short ride back to his uncle's home.

Lamb's alleged confusion as to where he was and shock at finding himself holding a shotgun while standing in the doorway of Anne Heaton's home led Dolan to conclude Lamb "was coming out of an 'acute psychotic episode' and 'returning to sanity'…as he stood inside the doorway of the Heaton home." Dolan believed Lamb's "return to sanity" explained the decision to not shoot Mrs Heaton. He concluded Lamb was divorced from reality when he gunned down his four victims, suffering from a "disease of the mind"—without naming or explaining the disease—and like Yaworsky, Dolan declared Lamb "incapable of appreciating the consequences of his actions." Lamb would later also tell his attorney, Saul Nosanchuk, that he had "tossed away the gun in a field, horrified to find himself holding the weapon," disposing of the shotgun in a haphazard manner just to be rid of it. The discarded-weapon story fit nicely with the psychiatric consensus that Lamb's sanity had returned while he was confronting Mrs Heaton.

The crime scene evidence tells a different story. Had these psychiatrists known or inquired with the Windsor Police about how the gun was found, this theory would have come apart. Sergeant Frank Chauvin's officers had found the gun placed, with ammunition carefully lined up, in what appeared to be an improvised sniper's nest. Certainly not haphazard or frenzied. Neither Yaworsky nor Dolan appear to have consulted Lamb's past criminal or personal history for their evaluations. Lamb had a pattern of escalating crimes of violence against strangers that might have given pause when considering the truthfulness of Lamb's claims.

***

Lamb's erratic behaviour—an energetic, seemingly manic performance to Yaworsky and the calculated storytelling given to

Dolan—points to a deeper debate that is still waged today: Can violent psychopaths claim that "my brain made me do it" as a defence? In essence, this is what Lamb was performing. As early as 1960, the *American Journal of Psychiatry* cited a major study assessing the criminal responsibility of murderers and the classification of "sane" or "insane" as features in their crimes. The sane murderer kills for rational, if highly unethical, reasons: robbery, silencing of witnesses, personal revenge, etc. The insane murderer kills for irrational reasons, usually driven by hallucinations or delusions or other symptoms of psychosis present during the commission of their crimes. An example of the "legally insane" psychotic murderer is Herbert Mullin, an honour student turned serial killer who terrorized California in the 1970s. Mullin believed his killing of thirteen people prevented large earthquakes from destroying the state, justifying his actions as a necessary public service—a kind of twisted homage to primitive societies who appeased their gods by tossing live virgins into active volcanoes to prevent future eruptions. He explained his homicides by claiming each victim telepathically communicated to Mullin their willingness to be "sacrificed" just prior to their murder. Although found guilty of first-degree murder at the time, there is now understanding and substantial evidence that Mullin suffered from schizophrenia, a brain disease that produces hallucinations as it eats away at the organic brain material.

In his classic book *Mindhunter,* John Douglas, co-founder of the FBI's Behavioural Science Unit at Quantico acknowledges that high-functioning serial and spree killers suffer from the mental illness classified as "psychopathic personality disorder," yet are "consciously aware their violent crimes are both 'morally wrong' and illegal." Douglas argues that just because they are psychopaths doesn't mean they don't know what they were doing when they were doing it, and in no way excuses them from the legal consequences of their actions. The best forensic psychiatrists and criminal profilers agree that psychopaths who commit inexplicable violent crimes usually behave rationally in other aspects of their daily lives. Moreover, these offenders are not psychotic, nor is there any evidence they suffer "temporary psychotic episodes" during their crimes. Violent psychopathic offenders know exactly what they are doing when they are doing it. They do it because it feels good and fulfills some deep psychological need important to the offender's warped pathology. FBI agent John Douglas's vast first-hand experience dealing with abnormal criminal behaviour, supported by the forensic psychiatric evidence, conclusively demonstrates these types of killers are "in no way insane."

Douglas isn't the only one to come to this conclusion as academics and legal scholars continue to debate the relationship between psychopaths, culpability, and insanity. A 2018 study by Anneli Jefferson and Katrina Sifferd suggest that a diagnosis of psychopathy "does not generally indicate that a defendant is eligible for an insanity defence." They argue that there may be some psychopaths who do have significant mental impairments, but they are the exception. In fact, many psychopaths are "not incapacitated in a way relevant to responsibility."

For Matthew Charles Lamb, convincing the court of his insanity was a matter of life and death.

***

Upon receiving Dolan's pretrial psychiatric evaluation, the court ordered Lamb to undergo a third psychiatric assessment at the Oak Ridge Facility for the Criminally Insane at Penetanguishene, Ontario. This time, things went differently. On August 24, 1966, Lamb was returned to Windsor with a report from Oak Ridge confirming he was psychologically fit to stand trial and participate in his own defence. He was then moved to Windsor's Brock County Jail to await his upcoming trial on capital murder, while the Crown prosecutor and Lamb's defence team constructed competing narratives to sell to a jury tasked with deciding whether eighteen-year-old Lamb should be hospitalized in perpetuity or die for his crime.

CHAPTER SEVEN:

Homicide Pretrial Prep for Dummies

IN THE 1960S, ONTARIO DID HAVE A LEGAL AID system, but it operated differently than it does today. All low-income or indigent citizens had the right to competent legal representation in a court of law, but lawyers who provided assistance did so pro bono. The Windsor Legal Aid program was comprised of local attorneys volunteering their legal expertise free of charge, and being reimbursed by the Ontario government only for incidental expenses such as administrative costs and gas mileage. Windsor criminal attorneys participating in the program worked on a rotational basis, accepting a case when their turn came around. Lamb—newly released from federal prison—could ill afford to pay for a defence lawyer and was subsequently assigned legal representation.

In 1966, Justice Saul Nosanchuk was a young and ambitious criminal lawyer born and raised in Windsor, and an active volunteer with the Legal Aid program. A newspaper photograph of Nosanchuk from this period depicts a tall and physically fit young man wearing a suit and tie, with short, neatly cropped black hair and a face dominated by black-rimmed eyeglasses. When asked if he'd be interested in defending Lamb as a legal aid client, Nosanchuk eagerly agreed, knowing this case would challenge his legal skills and courtroom performance under pressure as defence attorney, in a high-stakes murder trial that guaranteed wide media coverage. When I interviewed him, Saul Nosanchuk was seventy-nine years of age,[3] and had a long and distinguished career to look back on—as a successful criminal attorney until 1976, when he was called to the bench; he then served honourably as a magistrate of the Ontario Court of Justice for twenty-seven years:

> I originally wanted to be a sociologist or psychologist
> and received my Bachelor's Degree in the social sciences,
> but soon realized this wasn't for me, so I attended
> Osgoode [Hall] Law School in Toronto and was called
> to the bar in 1959. I returned to Windsor to set up my
> private practice in criminal law.

His empathy for people and commitment to fairness pervades all his conversations. Criminal offenders fortunate enough to have appeared in Justice Nosanchuk's court always received a fair hearing with all aspects of their case duly considered before a judgment was rendered. In talking to Nosanchuk at length, it becomes apparent this man could find a redeeming feature in the most despicable human being—a good quality for a court magistrate.

Even with his advanced age, Nosanchuk clearly recalled every name and detail pertaining to the Matthew Lamb case as if it had happened only yesterday. Prior to deciding on a defence strategy or entertaining a possible plea bargain with the prosecution, he had to obtain Lamb's written consent to represent him, a formality to which Lamb readily agreed. Nosanchuk's first

---

3   Saul Nosanchuk passed away on June 19, 2017, at the age of eighty-three.

impression of Lamb concurs with most people's first impressions of the defendant: boyish in appearance and of average height; thin but handsome; and well spoken, polite.

In their first attorney-client consultation, Lamb's detailed recollection of the murders admitted to Dr Dolan and the Oak Ridge psychiatrists vanished once again into ambiguities and evasiveness. When Nosanchuk pressed him about the events on the night of the murders, Lamb came across "as a somewhat confused and tentative individual, conveying the impression he was not really involved in the shootings"—but if he was, "he had not wanted to participate in them." After talking for a while, Lamb took another approach, admitting to Nosanchuk that he dimly recalled watching a violent John Wayne movie at his uncle's home that night. Lamb went on to share his belief that it influenced his decision to proceed with the spree, while at the same time insisting he was "still not entirely sure he had committed the killings." Contradictions and head games aside, Lamb gave Nosanchuk the impression he was unconcerned by the seriousness of the charges against him and the possibility of execution if convicted, leaving Nosanchuk to conclude "Lamb was quite prepared to let justice take its course."

As a defence attorney, Nosanchuk's primary duty was keeping Lamb's neck out of the hangman's noose. There was no doubt Lamb was responsible for the shotgun killings of Edith Chaykoski and Andrew Woloch and the wounding of Kenneth Chaykoski and Grace Dunlop. Nosanchuk knew there was no chance of Crown Prosecutor Eugene Duchesne agreeing to a guilty plea bargain on two counts of manslaughter. Lamb's crime was far too egregious for that. He also decided against arguing mitigating circumstances, such as drunkenness, which might challenge the prosecution's contention that Lamb intended to use the shotgun to cause serious harm or death—as proof of intent was necessary for a capital-murder conviction. Nosanchuk decided an insanity defence offered the only possible chance of winning an acquittal. Failure would condemn his young client to death.

Nosanchuk began preparing the defence case by investigating Lamb's childhood, interviewing family members and friends. He learned of Lamb's parental abandonment while still an infant; the absence of affection from his extended family, including many who made it clear they viewed Lamb as an unwanted burden; and of Lamb's physical and verbal abuse suffered at the hands of his step-grandfather. Parental abandonment and lack of love and nurturing as a child certainly contributed to the development of Lamb's psychopathic personality. Nosanchuk realized, of course, that the prosecution would argue that thousands of other children are born into loveless deprivation and conditions far worse than Lamb's, yet do not grow up to be violent offenders. He would need more ammunition than Lamb's tragic past to win the most difficult and statistically least successful of defence pleas: not guilty by reason of insanity.

Nosanchuk still expresses his anger and disgust with Lamb having been sentenced to two years in a federal penitentiary for the robbery and shootout at Lakeview Marine on Christmas Eve of 1964: "Imagine sentencing a sixteen-year-old boy to Kingston Penitentiary for a crime in which no one was hurt," he remarked indignantly. The counterargument suggests the sentencing judge considered what the consequences would have been had Lamb been a better shot when he opened fire on OPP Officer Cail Miller and Bernie Desjardins, and of Lamb's prior and unprovoked attack on Constable Graham outside the Riverside Arena earlier that same year. Surprisingly, Nosanchuk admits he didn't know the specific details of the 1964 Lakeview robbery, then or now, and was surprised to learn Lamb had prepared an ambush in a well-concealed gully, waiting for police officers to arrive and investigate his break-in.

Nosanchuk carefully reviewed Lamb's psychiatric evaluations submitted to the court by Dr Walter Yaworsky and Dr James Dolan regarding the shooting spree of June 25, 1966. Yaworsky told Nosanchuk of his surprise at the defendant's lack of concern regarding the killings. He recounted Lamb's obfuscating and frequent changing of the subject, his grandiose statements, and claims of amnesia regarding the shootings. Yaworsky told the defence attorney he believed Lamb's claim of amnesia was sincere, citing Lamb's story of "how he [Lamb] thought it strange to find himself in a taxi returning to his uncle's home," with no memory of the shootings he'd committed just minutes earlier. Yaworsky believed Lamb's flimsy and fragile personality structure was responsible for a "psychotic break with reality" during the shootings, and that it was "not likely Lamb was putting on an act." The doctor cited Lamb's psychopathic personality for the cause of his failing to "appreciate the nature of his crime" and concluded he was, therefore, "criminally insane." Nosanchuk identified two key points in Yaworsky's analysis essential to convincing a jury Lamb met the criteria of legal insanity: Lamb's "amnesia" triggered by a "psychotic break" during the shootings, and Lamb's "inability to appreciate the nature of his crime" due to a psychopathic personality disorder. "I wanted this psychiatrist to testify," Nosanchuk said, "as he was the first psychiatrist to evaluate Lamb's state of mind just two days after the shootings." Yaworsky subsequently agreed to testify for the defence.

Two days before Lamb's murder trial began, Yaworsky was urgently summoned to the jailhouse where Lamb told the doctor that he remembered more about the shootings. Lamb revealed that "he had found himself standing in Anne Heaton's living room with no clear idea how he got there on the night of the shootings." Further, Lamb said how "shocked" he was to find himself holding a shotgun in his hand, which he quickly threw away after running out of the Heaton residence. Lamb knew Yaworsky was testifying for the defence. Was he reinforcing a version of events to support his plea of temporary insanity?

Nosanchuk next interviewed Dr Dolan of St. Thomas Ontario Psychiatric Hospital. Dolan admitted Lamb recalled the precise details of the shootings—only two days after claiming amnesia to Yaworsky. Yet this contradiction didn't prevent Dolan from agreeing with Yaworsky's conclusion that Lamb had suffered a "psychotic break" during the shootings. Dolan believed that Lamb "regained his sanity" when confronting, but not shooting, Anne Heaton at her Westminster home. Dolan also agreed to testify for the defence at Lamb's trial.

On the night before his murder trial began, Lamb requested Dolan visit him at the county jail, just as Yaworsky had been summoned the previous night. Lamb whispered in Dolan's ear how he heard "all kinds of strange voices in his cell at night, like toilets flushing" at the county jail where he was being held pending trial. The timing of this information, as was his revelation to Yaworsky, is certainly suspect. Lamb was painting a picture of himself as unstable, prone to bouts of "episodic psychosis." Lamb's last-minute summoning of both doctors can be seen as further manipulation of professional witnesses by the defendant.

Nosanchuk next reviewed the reports of the five psychiatrists who evaluated Lamb at the Oak Ridge Facility for the Criminally Insane at Penetanguishene. All five psychiatrists concluded Lamb "understood what he was doing when he carried out the killings, that Lamb knew he had loaded the gun, knew he fired the gun, and 'knew his actions were wrong'." The five psychiatrists "unanimously dismissed" Lamb's claims of amnesia told to, and believed by, Dr Yaworsky. The Oak Ridge psychiatrists had ample experience interacting with the psychopathic personality, yet were divided as to the degree to which Lamb's psychopathic personality affected his ability to "appreciate the consequences of his actions" on the night of the shootings. Three of the five psychiatrists—Dr George Darby, Dr Barry Boyd, and Dr Elliott T. Barker—were of the opinion that Lamb knew his murderous assault was wrong. However, they believed that his emotional fragility and immaturity, combined with his insufficient empathy for others, rendered Lamb incapable of "truly appreciating" the nature and consequences of killing another human being. These three psychiatrists agreed to testify for the defence.

Dr Basil Orchard, who also evaluated Lamb at Oak Ridge, was having none of it. Dr Orchard concluded Lamb knew exactly what he was doing when he shot Edith Chaykoski, Andrew Woloch, Kenneth Chaykoski, and Grace Dunlop and, moreover, appreciated the consequences of his actions. During his examination of the defendant, Orchard caught Lamb telling a number of lies and was convinced Lamb made up various stories for different psychiatrists to avoid responsibility for his murder rampage. Orchard would only agree to testify for the prosecution.

Supporting Orchard's opinion of Lamb, Dr Wilfred Boothroyd, a renowned senior psychiatrist at Sunnybrook Hospital in Toronto reviewed all the police, psychiatric, and psychological reports on Lamb and on the circumstances pertaining to the June 25 shootings. Boothroyd concluded Lamb knew he was shooting human beings, knew right from wrong, appreciated the nature and consequences of killing other human beings, and was criminally responsible for his actions. Nosanchuk conceded Drs Orchard and Boothroyd would make strong prosecution witnesses for Crown Attorney Eugene Duchesne, as both psychiatrists had impeccable credentials working with violent psychopaths and paranoid schizophrenics. Both men held diametrically opposite views from their three Penetanguishene colleagues testifying for the defence, but only on the question of the degree to which the impact of Lamb's psychopathy affected his ability to "appreciate" the consequences of his shooting spree.

Nosanchuk also consulted Dr George Scott, director of psychiatry at Kingston Penitentiary, who had evaluated Lamb in prison and expressed concern over Lamb's elaborate fantasies involving fights, shootings, and killings—all indicators of Lamb's pent-up hostility. Dr Scott stated in his prison psychiatric evaluation that he "wasn't sure" whether Lamb was really exhibiting signs of developing a hypomanic illness or "just faking it." Despite his strong reservations, Scott nevertheless agreed to Lamb's early release from prison—just seventeen days before his killing spree. "I considered Dr Scott a 'controversial' witness,"

Nosanchuk admits, "because he had signed off on Lamb's release from Kingston Penitentiary but gambled on Dr Scott's impressive and authoritative bearing making a strong impression on a jury." Scott agreed to testify for the defence.

***

Nosanchuk likely sensed that the uniqueness of Lamb's crime would work in favour of an insanity defence. The strangeness of Lamb's murder spree was such a rare anomaly in the 1960s. Today, school shootings and shopping-mall massacres are routinely reported by the mainstream media for a day or two, before disappearing into the ethereal emptiness of an apathetic public. Today's spree killers are virtually guaranteed guilty convictions, based on scholarly consensus that in the majority of cases, a violent psychopath is a legally sane offender with a personality disorder. Moreover, *spree killer* and *serial killer* were non-existent terms in the 1960s. Robert Ressler, Roy Hazelwood, and John Douglas, the founding members of the FBI's Behavioural Science Unit at Quantico, Virginia, coined these terms to define and categorize these two new types of multiple-homicide offenders whose numbers had exploded exponentially by the early 1970s.

Contrary to popular belief, in the courtroom *insanity* is a legal term, not a psychiatric one. The Canadian Criminal Code, Section 16(2), states: "A person is 'insane' when he has a disease of the mind to an extent that renders him incapable of 'appreciating' the nature and quality of an act or omission, or 'knowing' that an act or omission was 'wrong'." Psychiatrists and psychologists are nevertheless essential for determining whether a criminal's behaviour meets the legal criteria in insanity-plea cases. Nosanchuk was concerned about the pretrial psychiatric reports of Dr Dolan and the five psychiatrists from the Oak Ridge Facility. All five doctors said Lamb recalled his shooting rampage quite clearly—Lamb's claims of amnesia told (or sold) to Dr Yaworsky notwithstanding—facts that did not bode well for a successful insanity defence. "I knew there was enough evidence for the Crown prosecutor to convict Lamb of capital murder when going with the insanity plea," Nosanchuk admits, "but I believed the psychiatric evidence I could put before a jury was strong enough to win an acquittal because the law required that Lamb 'appreciate the consequences' of his actions at the time he committed the shootings." Therein lies the rub.

Nosanchuk's challenge to winning an acquittal for Lamb would be twofold. First, the defence had to convince a jury that Lamb was incapable of appreciating the nature, consequences, and wrongness of his crime. Nosanchuk would produce psychiatric testimony arguing Lamb also suffered a "temporary psychotic or hypomanic break" during the shootings, causing acute mental confusion—as evidence of Lamb's inability to appreciate the consequences of his homicidal actions. Should the "hypomanic break" theory posited by the defence prove unconvincing at trial, Nosanchuk would have to rely on convincing a jury that Lamb's psychopathy alone prevented him from "appreciating" the consequences of his crimes. To win his case, Nosanchuk needed his defence psychiatrists to prove more persuasive to a trial jury than Crown Prosecutor Eugene Duchesne's psychiatric expert witnesses, in addition to police testimony and witnesses the prosecution would introduce at trial.

Nosanchuk was backed up against the wall as the trial date neared, pursuing an insanity defence as his only chance for an acquittal. Considering the difficulty of winning insanity-defence cases, I asked Nosanchuk why he didn't propose a deal to Prosecutor Eugene Duchesne and plead Lamb guilty to two counts of second-degree murder (murder without prior intent), which carried a sentence of ten to twenty years before the possibility of parole. Sensing my skepticism of his willingness to risk a death sentence for his client—in a murder trial based entirely on the subjectivity of psychiatric testimony and unpredictable jurors—Nosanchuk sat back in his chair, bared that sly smile of his, and said:

I felt we had the psychiatric evidence necessary to win with an insanity defence. You see, in 1967, "insanity" was determined by the *quantity* of psychiatric probabilities and the Lamb case was unique in that all three Oak Ridge psychiatrists who agreed to testify for the defence agreed that Lamb recalled the events of the killings that night, but were all of the opinion Lamb's mental illness precluded him from "fully appreciating" the nature of his acts, of the taking of human life, and was incapable of showing remorse for his victims.

Nosanchuk continued: "My defence had to emphasize Lamb was mentally ill with a psychopathic personality that mitigated his responsibility to where it met Canada's Criminal Code definition of 'legal insanity'."

Pausing for a few moments to allow me to absorb his strategic reasoning for defending Lamb, Nosanchuk just sat back in his chair, smiling, before flatly admitting: "To tell you the truth, I just decided to go for broke." In 1967, given the mandatory penalty of death by hanging should Lamb be convicted, this was a risky and gutsy strategy for Nosanchuk to take.

Nosanchuk briefly considered having Lamb take the stand, but quickly decided against it. Defence psychiatrists would be arguing Lamb suffered an "acute psychotic episode" during his killing spree, while Dr Scott of Kingston Penitentiary would testify Lamb had "spent his entire life living in a fantasy world" and "was out of touch with reality" during the shootings. Nosanchuk knew Lamb's rational demeanour was the antithesis of insanity and would undermine his case if Lamb testified in his own defence. Nosanchuk's careful portrait of an immature, irrational, part-time psychotic spree killer would be dismantled as soon as an articulate and intelligent Lamb took the stand. Moreover, a cross-examination of Lamb by the prosecutor could be wildly unpredictable. Nosanchuk was smart enough not to take that risk.

On December 10, 1966, just three weeks before Lamb's capital-murder trial, a suspicious and timely incident occurred at the Brock County Jail where Lamb was incarcerated, providing the defence with additional evidence that Lamb was mentally unstable and prone to irrational violent eruptions for no apparent reasons. Aware of his impending trial, Lamb performed a reprise of the devil's dance for his jailers. He proceeded to set fire to his blankets and mattress, broke "more than a hundred windows," and damaged the building's plumbing, causing a flood at the jail. Lamb's jailhouse performance lasted three hours and had its intended result. Governor Robinson, officer in charge of the County Jail, reported that throughout the summer and fall of 1966, Lamb had been a model prisoner, which made his sudden outburst that December all the more astonishing. Governor Robinson was shocked by Lamb's unprovoked violence. Nosanchuk recognized the value of Lamb's jailhouse fit to his insanity defence. Robinson was persuaded to testify for the defence at Lamb's upcoming trial.

***

Crown Prosecutor Eugene Duchesne is remembered by Windsor Police officers as a very astute and experienced litigator with an almost textbook memory for case law precedent and its application in criminal cases. Duchesne was also gifted with the actor's ability to match emotion with legal rhetoric which all juries find so persuasive. Duchesne's professionalism and trial experience made him a formidable opponent to Nosanchuk's high-risk gamble to win an acquittal for Lamb on an insanity plea.

During the dying days of 1966, Duchesne and Nosanchuk reviewed their trial notes and tied up any loose ends for their upcoming court battle. Competing psychiatric theories, based largely on speculation and subjective professional opinion, would be the decisive weapons used to determine Lamb's fate. Nosanchuk believed he could win an acquittal for Lamb based on mental instability while Duchesne was equally confident he could parry those defence thrusts with his own psychiatric wit-nesses—supported by police and witness testimony—and a trial jury's instinctive unwillingness to see a remorseless killer escape punishment for such a heinous crime. Duchesne knew he had a strong case and was confident of convicting Lamb, followed by the obligatory death sentence.

A key factor in Lamb's 1967 capital-murder trial would be the non-observance of rules of disclosure in Canadian law, which today requires prosecutors to turn over all of their case evidence to defence counsel before trial. Duchesne's prosecutorial files con-tained all witness statements, police reports, psychiatric assess-ments, and material evidence the prosecution might introduce at Lamb's trial. In 1967, the prosecutor was not required to disclose evidence—an advantage that prosecutors no longer enjoy under Canadian criminal law. Nevertheless, the "burden of proof" of guilt in 1967, like today, lay entirely with the prosecution.

Windsor's legal community was a small, elite group with strong social ties. The turnover of prosecution files to the defence was strictly a voluntary affair, perhaps requested by a defence attor-ney while planning an upcoming golf game with the Crown pros-ecutor. Nosanchuk had some foreknowledge of Duchesne's trial strategy based on educated assumptions and his prior experience, yet was unaware of the witnesses the prosecution would introduce at trial. Nosanchuk enjoyed the same privilege by denying pretrial defence information to the Crown.

Everything was now set for Lamb's capital-murder trial. In a bizarre coincidence, Lamb would have to share media attention with Richard Speck, as their trial dates were set for the same week. Only 480 kilometres separated the Chicago and Windsor court-rooms, and while the American mainstream media now spent more ink on the Speck killings, which they dubbed THE CRIME OF THE CENTURY, the Detroit media would still report on Lamb's trial. Speck would be found guilty of all charges and spend the rest of his life in prison. Speck, like Charles Whitman after him, claimed more victims than Lamb, but Lamb's rampage was the initial spark that ignited the widely publicized—and poorly understood—spree killer phenomenon during the summer of 1966. Further, the post-offense fates of Whitman and Speck pale into insignificance compared with that of Canadian spree killer Matthew Charles Lamb, whose post-trial saga was, and remains, unique in the annals of rampage killers.

CHAPTER EIGHT:

A Trial of Errors

IT WAS A CHILLY MORNING ON JANUARY 16, 1967, when the capital-murder trial of the Crown vs. Matthew Charles Lamb commenced. Justice Alexander Stark of the Supreme Court of Ontario was presiding. The trial would last only five days, but its ramifications would echo into Canadian case law for years to come.

The provincial government's decision to appoint Justice Stark to adjudicate the Lamb trial was a controversial choice. Stark had been a business attorney for the *Toronto Star,* one of Canada's leading newspapers. Appointed to the Ontario Supreme Court less than a year before Lamb's murder trial, Stark had no background in criminal law or trial experience, having never presided over a criminal trial or rendered sole judgment on so much as a parking ticket. Nevertheless, the Ontario government assigned Stark to sit in judgment for this rarest of crimes in the 1960s: the high-profile capital-murder trial of a rampage killer. Saul Nosanchuk later wrote of Stark as a fair, competent, and highly regarded legal professional. This may well have been true in Stark's field of business or libel law, but when I asked if Stark's appointment to the Ontario Supreme Court had been a patronage appointment engineered by Toronto's Bay Street elites, Nosanchuk just smiled. "You suggested that, not me."

Stark opened the trial proceedings with the unusual decision to allow psychiatrists testifying for both the prosecution and the defence to remain in the courtroom throughout the trial, where they could hear the testimony of their colleagues and opponents before they themselves took the stand. Standing behind the defence table alongside Nosanchuk, Lamb looked dapper with a fresh haircut and new clothes: a handsome, clean-cut young man any protective father would approve as his daughter's high school prom date. Also standing at the defence table was Brian Clements, Nosanchuk's junior defence co-counsel, taking part in his first criminal trial. Clements was a promising young criminal attorney who would himself be one day appointed a justice of the Ontario Supreme Court.

To begin the trial, Lamb, then nineteen years of age, stood before the magistrate and entered his plea of "not guilty" for the capital murder of Edith Chaykoski in a "clear, steady" voice, according to the *Windsor Star* journalist in attendance. The defence then informed the court they would "invoke the 'insanity defence' under Section 16 (2) of the Canadian Criminal Code."

Nosanchuk strode over to the jury box. Windsor Police officers who worked closely with Nosanchuk during his years as a defence attorney and as a magistrate hold him in high regard, but laughingly recall how his hands would often visibly shake from fear whenever he argued a case in court. However, when it was his turn to orate, he would miraculously transform into a smooth-talking, confident, persuasive attorney. This is the commanding presence that the jury were about to meet.

Nosanchuk opened by telling jurors he would produce psychiatric testimony proving Lamb suffered from a mental illness that did not allow the defendant to "fully appreciate" the consequences of his actions, and that Lamb's fragile personality had triggered a psychotic breakdown leaving him temporarily insane during the shootings. Nosanchuk knew the defence's case would rise or fall on the strength of the psychiatric testimony. He carefully painted a picture for the jury of a dysfunctional young man whose childhood deprivations and violent fantasies manifested into a dangerous, uncontrollable mental disorder. On that fateful night, June 25, 1966, Lamb's inner rage escalated into true madness. Based on this, Nosanchuk would be asking the trial jury to judge Lamb not guilty on the basis of insanity.

Eugene Duchesne, Crown attorney and chief prosecutor for Lamb's capital-murder trial, was an experienced criminal lawyer with a brilliant legal mind but he could not match Nosanchuk's charisma in the courtroom. However, his team was strengthened by a strong legal adviser. His mentor, Justice Bruce Macdonald, was a former prosecutor and Second World War veteran who helped prosecute and convict Nazi Regimental Commander Kurt Meyer of the 12th SS Jugend Panzer Division for illegally executing twenty Canadian POWs near Caen, France, in June 1944—just two days after the successful D-Day landings. Judge Macdonald would later be appointed to the Ontario Supreme Court. Retired Windsor Police detectives Al Proctor and Don Cushman recall Macdonald as a "real bulldog" in court. Macdonald brought all that weight to bear on Duchesne. All prosecutors understand their careers are evaluated by the number of convictions they obtain, and Duchesne already had an impressive collection before Lamb's murder trial.

Duchesne's opening statement to the court portrayed Lamb as a sadistic and cruel killer with the presence of mind to take out his uncle's shotgun, load it, then hide behind a tree waiting for six pedestrians walking up Ford Boulevard, before jumping out onto the sidewalk and opening fire. Duchesne told the court of Lamb's initial denials of having committed the shootings until overwhelming evidence forced Lamb to conditionally admit to his crime. This was proof of a calculating, cunning, and rational mind "fully aware of the consequences of his actions," and possessing the intellectual ability to later con professional psychiatrists with various fabricated tales designed to feign "insanity." Although Duchesne restated the false account of Lamb waiting to ambush six pedestrians in his opening statement to the jury, his mention of Lamb hiding his gun after the shootings suggested the prosecution would handily discredit the defence's version of events on the evening of June 25, 1966.

***

It is a fact that prosecution and defence attorneys prepare their witnesses for jury trials. Witnesses are instructed how to present their testimony in court, which points to emphasize during questioning, what questions they can expect to be asked under cross-examination, and how to respond to them. Most witnesses, including police officers, seldom lie but will sometimes embellish their court testimony to help attain a desired verdict. Witnesses are human beings with an innate need to project a favourable impression of themselves onto others—whether they are educated professionals, police officers, or unemployed drifters. Everyone wants their testimony to matter to the jury and make a difference in deliberations, especially in a high-stakes homicide trial with wide media coverage. The Lamb murder trial provided a platform for medical professionals to espouse their psychiatric opinions and theories before a large audience, and other witnesses likely enjoyed the recognition of their names appearing in the newspaper—a realization of their fifteen minutes of fame.

Lamb's uncle Stanley Hasketh took the stand as the first prosecution witness. He described his horror at finding the strewn shotgun shells, empty ammunition box, and missing shotgun, shaking his nephew from a deep sleep to demand an answer. He questioned Lamb about the deadly shootings just down the street. According to Hasketh, Lamb was at first evasive, but eventually admitted he "didn't know what happened but he must have done it," and eventually, he "had probably shot some people."

The survivors of Lamb's attack that night got their day in court. Now the victims each took the stand, staring down their attacker, sitting calm and collected just a few metres away. Charmaine Chaykoski had been the only one who was able to identify the defendant out of a police lineup. The other survivors in their walking party described Lamb's demeanour in the moments before he opened fire. "He was just like anyone else talking. There was no emotion at all," declared Kenneth Chaykoski—who had been wounded by Lamb's bullets. Vincent Franco added that the voice of the gunman "wasn't overwhelmed with emotion; it was fairly cool," and Don Mulesa only echoed this, saying the man "spoke coldly and harshly with no sign of emotion I could see." Even the taxi driver, William Robinson, who picked up Lamb at Remington Park and drove him right past the crime scene to 1912 Ford, testified that "the man didn't show any interest in the commotion [...] was very quiet during the short ride." He detected no alcohol on the young man who sat in his back seat.

The prosecution brought this parade of witnesses, with very similar testimonies, as a strategy. Duchesne wanted to convince the jury Lamb was mission-oriented and in complete control of his faculties throughout his murder rampage—a rational killer committing an irrational act to satisfy his sadistic impulses, regardless of the consequences.

Rising to cross-examine the first prosecution witnesses, Nosanchuk charged out of the gate playing offence. With his line of questioning, Nosanchuk persuaded these first prosecution witnesses to agree with the defence argument that Lamb's calm manner during the shootings could also be interpreted as a disturbed young man appearing "distant" and "unaware" of what was going on around him. Nosanchuk actually convinced one prosecution witness to state "Lamb was so oblivious of his surroundings he [Lamb] even failed to notice a party in progress in a garage across the street." Surprisingly, neither the defence nor the prosecution challenged the witness's erroneous location of the "garage party," as the shootings occurred directly in front of said party. Moreover, Duchesne did not use his right to redirect or requestion the prosecution witnesses after the defence's cross-examination. By failing to challenge his own witnesses, Duchesne allowed the ambiguity of Lamb's state of mind during the shootings to resonate with the jury.

Police officers testifying to Lamb's calm demeanour, both during and after his arrest, partially salvaged Duchesne's portrayal of Lamb as a cool, calculating killer. The defence chose not to challenge the police testimony, knowing full well law officers would better recognize the courtroom ploy the defence successfully used on prosecution eyewitnesses. Other witnesses were brought in to speak to the brutality of the crime. Detective Edward Charles Hunt carefully described a mundane detail: Edith Chaykoski's purse. He was given the bag at the hospital upon her death, and noted the powder burns and a nickle-sized hole through it. He also recovered two 16-gauge spent shotgun shells from the scene on Ford Boulevard. Pathologist William Harold Stanley Asselstine described how he picked thirty-one pellets from Chaykoski's pelvis, and stated her cause of death as bleeding out from a wound in her abdomen. He told the jury that the shot had to have been fired from close range, "because wadding doesn't travel too far with its light weight." Despite these harrowing details, it became clear by the end of the first day of testimony that the battle of competing narratives presented by the prosecution and defence would make Lamb's mental state during his killing spree the primary focus of the trial.

***

When Anne Heaton of 1793 Westminster took the stand for the prosecution, her testimony had changed from her initial police statement given to Sergeant Frank Chauvin on the morning after the shootings. She began by reiterating that Lamb threatened to shoot her, then forced his way into her living room, but now she told the court how Lamb gazed about her home, then "suddenly looked frightened" and "ran out into the night" after she called out for her husband. Originally, Heaton had told Chauvin—and Detective Sergeant Jim Ure when he interviewed her—that Lamb failed to react, seemingly ignoring her threat, and lingered before walking out of her house and heading toward her backyard and the open fields beyond.

Why these key details in Heaton's testimony shifted is unclear. It may have been as simple as nerves about testifying in court or embellishing pertinent facts. However, this subtle but profound change meant that Heaton's testimony did more to contribute to the defence than the prosecution. It played right into the defence's portrayal of a delusional young man emerging from a "psychotic break" and "coming to his senses" while inside the Heaton home. Importantly, Duchesne either failed to realize this change or decided not to challenge her testimony. It became apparent that the prosecution faced an uphill battle.

***

It was time for the defence witnesses to take the stand. Nosanchuk had prepare an onslaught of experts, and first up was Dr Walter Yaworsky, the Windsor psychiatrist who encountered Lamb at the county jail just two days after the killing spree. The doctor testified he "felt" Lamb was "completely insane" on the night of the shooting. "He went for the gun with thoughts of killing himself—he'd tried it in the past—and then dashed out into the street," the psychiatrist told the court. In fact, Yaworsky believed Lamb—then claiming total amnesia—was still insane at the time of their interview, when Lamb claimed total amnesia, adding that Lamb "suffered an 'acute psychotic reaction' in a psychopathic personality." He described how Lamb had passionately declared that he would "kill himself if he found out that he had actually committed the shootings." But when Yaworsky told him of Edith Chaykoski's death, Lamb whispered, "Poor broad," and giggled.

In my interview with him, Nosanchuk admitted that he had coached Yaworsky to emphasize Lamb's giggling upon hearing of Edith Chaykoski's death to help convince jurors of Lamb's mental instability. The result was better than Nosanchuk anticipated. The young defendant had been eerily emotionless up to this point in the trial, but when Yaworsky testified to his reaction to Chaykoski's death, he let out a giggle right there in the courtroom—his first audible reaction three days into the trial. Whether Lamb's giggling in court was involuntary or contrived for effect is unclear, but it could only help the defence's insanity argument.

Duchesne came out from behind the prosecutor's table to vigorously challenge Dr Yaworsky:

"You testified Lamb was at that time divorced from reality, completely insane?"

"Yes," Yaworsky replied, adding how Lamb seemed to remember more of that night when the psychiatrist again spoke with the defendant in December 1966 and again just two days before the trial was scheduled to begin. "He [Lamb] now recalls confronting some people, but everything went 'fuzzy' when pulling the trigger," Yaworsky recalled from his final interview with the defendant. "Lamb also told me his memory of the shootings was now clearer than before [...] 'I remember standing in the Heatons' living room when all of a sudden I looked down and there was a gun in my hand. That's when I ran out!" Yaworsky told the court he "believed Lamb's 'sanity' returned at this point." The doctor then quickly added, "Lamb's acute psychotic reaction 'didn't have to be triggered by an external set of events' and it 'could have come from something deep inside'."

"Isn't it possible," Duchesne countered, "that Lamb, who has an intelligence quotient of 125, could have sold you a bill of goods during your first June interview?"

"I don't think so," Yaworsky replied, adding how "Lamb's psychopathic behaviour was enough to justify 'insanity' even if Lamb didn't suffer an 'acute psychotic episode'."

In other words, Yaworsky was equating psychopathy with insanity—revealing that it shouldn't matter if Lamb was truly in a psychotic episode or even faked his amnesia.

Duchesne knew he must discredit the defence's psychiatric witnesses if he was to convict Lamb of capital murder, yet the prosecutor missed many opportunities to poke holes in the expert testimony. He didn't question if Yaworsky had administered any psychiatric tests or narrow in on the doctor's original report, particularly the line that Yaworsky "didn't think Lamb was faking his symptoms." Bringing statements like this to the jury's attention might place doubt in Yaworksy's judgment and conclusions. Further, the psychiatrist alleged that Lamb had tried to commit suicide while in Kingston Penitentiary, but there's no record of an attempt on his life while incarcerated. The only physical evidence was a few superficial scratches on his arm. Neither is there a record of Lamb attempting suicide while waiting seven months in the Brock County Jail for his capital-murder trial to begin. This may seem like a low blow, but any opportunity that the prosecution could take to show that Lamb had lied to the psychiatrist, and more important, that Yaworsky believed it, would be invaluable to the jury.

Dr James Dolan, clinical director of psychiatry at the St. Thomas Ontario Psychiatric Hospital, was called to the stand next. To a hushed audience, he revealed that he had interviewed Lamb again the night before the trial began, and that Lamb now "remembered all about the night of the shootings." Unlike with Yaworsky, Lamb had never claimed full amnesia to Dolan in earlier interviews, but he still proceeded to reveal new details of that night. The *Windsor Star* ran with this revelation as their article header—signalling how the doctor's words must have fallen on the audience.

According to Dolan, Lamb described "feeling as if someone else was committing the crimes like on television, as if he was invisible," while acknowledging he knew he was the shooter. "Everything seemed unreal and the next memory was of confronting an old lady in a nearby house," he continued. "All the time, I was thinking, 'What the hell am I here for?'" Dolan now believed this was the exact moment that "Lamb returned to the real world...following a 'psychotic break'...divorcing him from reality." The psychiatrist ended his testimony with a diagnosis: Lamb suffered from a disease of the mind that rendered him incapable of appreciating the nature and quality of the act of killing another human being.

Duchesne took a similar cross approach with Dolan, focusing on Lamb's high intelligence and ability to concoct a story of losing touch with reality as an excuse for his desire to satisfy his sadistic impulses. Like Yaworsky, Dolan admitted in court the possibility that Lamb "made up his own story." Nevertheless, Dolan insisted his "clinical observations support Lamb was 'insane' at the time of his killings." He defined Lamb's "psychotic break" as emerging from his tortured personality and poor impulse control, leaving Lamb "unable to control himself" from committing his murder spree.

Nosanchuk next called Governor John Robinson, head of security at the Brock County Jail, to testify to Lamb's fragile and unpredictable mental state while awaiting trial. Robinson told the court about Lamb's surprising jailhouse rampage on December 19, 1966, when Lamb set fire to blankets, broke nearly "a hundred windows," and smashed plumbing fixtures to flood a jail cell. After three hours, Lamb was finally subdued by jail guards. "I was amazed at what I saw. Lamb's pupils were dilated like someone who comes into this jail heavy on narcotics, except their eyes look sunk in, while Lamb's eyes were bulging out of his head like a crazy person," Robinson recounted incredulously, as Lamb had been a model prisoner until this episode. How one skinny, unarmed prisoner was able to inflict this level of damage over such an extended period of time remained unquestioned and unanswered.

Nosanchuk admitted years later to his nervousness in put-ting his next witness, Dr George Scott, director of psychiatry at Kingston Penitentiary, on the stand. He recognized that Scott was in a vulnerable position. After all, the doctor had allowed Lamb's release from prison just seventeen days before his patient embarked on his killing spree. Even so, Nosanchuk considered Dr Scott's testimony too important to the defence's argument, as Scott would testify Lamb was "divorced from reality" during his killing spree.

Scott took the stand and told the court how Lamb lived in a fantasy world from the time he was a little boy. Matthew Lamb saw himself as an actor playing the part his emotions demanded, with-out appreciating the consequences. Psychiatric tests administered in prison showed Lamb to be an extremely immature young man fascinated by "the power of the gun." Scott conceded in court that Lamb's emotional state had been fragile, with signs of obvious mental breakdown, after being released from solitary confinement, where he'd been placed for fighting with another prisoner. "I didn't like being alone in the 'hole,'" Lamb had said. "It does things to a person."

In March 1966, after the mop-dragging incident, Scott placed Lamb in the prison hospital for three weeks of psychiatric observa-tion. The doctor explained to the court that Lamb rapidly improved, returned to the general population, and within three months was released on his recommendation—even though Scott believed that the young man was in a "pre-psychotic state." In Scott's view, a combination of factors provoked Lamb into a "full-blown schizoid episode." He admitted to the court that "prison officials were con-cerned for Lamb" and believed he was likely to reoffend.

"Then why did you let him out early?"

The voice of an angry young man cut through the quiet courtroom. It was Vincent Franco, leaping out of his seat to accuse the witness. In our interview years later, Franco still felt that frustration. "I couldn't stand listening anymore to the same garbage about how Lamb didn't feel bad for murdering his vic-tims and shouldn't be held accountable—all that crap they used to justify Lamb murdering my friends." Franco, a nineteen-year-old student barely out of high school, had shouted out the million-dollar question. A *Windsor Star* reporter wrote of the silence that descended upon the courtroom after Franco's outburst, and how "this vital question was left hanging in the air…unanswered."

Duchesne was chomping at the bit as he listened to Dr Scott testify. Jumping up from behind the prosecution table, he launched into a verbal attack. He demanded an answer to the same question that Franco had called out. How could Lamb have been given early release if federal prison officials believed he was a danger to society?

The doctor was ready. He argued that although Lamb was in a "marginal state of mental pathology," he was not "certifiably insane" at the time of release. When pressed by Duchesne on Lamb's psychiatric treatment during his three week-observation at the prison hospital, Scott defended himself, declaring that Lamb was "sick" when admitted, but soon "dropped his mental illness symptoms, so I felt I couldn't justify sending him to Penetanguishene Hospital for the Criminally Insane as Lamb displayed 'no 'florid' [obvious] symptoms." The prosecution let the matter rest there.

Years later, Saul Nosanchuk recalls how Scott—the witness he most feared placing on the stand because of his role in Lamb's release—made the greatest impact on the trial jury of all seven medical experts called for the defence. Scott maintained his composure and answered questions in an authoritative and convincing style. Detective Sergeant Jim Ure, chief investigator of the Lamb murder case, recalls his impression of Scott:

> That psychiatrist who came down from Kingston
> Penitentiary was the most impressive defence witness
> in my opinion. He said that the combination of factors
> such as Lamb's emotional state, the violent gunfights
> in a John Wayne television show Lamb watched on the
> night of the killings, coupled with Lamb's drinking
> about eight beers in that unbearable humid weather, all

came together in such a way that it set Lamb off on his shooting spree. I think Dr Scott made the most sense to the jury. Hell, I found myself half believing him.

At this point in the trial, Justice Stark called a short recess and Ure escorted Lamb to a temporary holding cell located next to the courtroom. Lamb and Ure had formed a grudgingly respectful relationship where both felt comfortable in each other's company. While waiting to return to the courtroom, Lamb gestured with his thumb in the direction of the courtroom and remarked to Ure:

> Those guys arguing in there are the crazy ones, not me.
> I'm fine. I know exactly what I'm doing…what I do.
> Yeah, they should be getting treatment instead of me.
> It's just that killing a stranger means nothing to me. To me, it feels just like stepping on a bug. That's all.

Lamb honestly admitted to Ure what he had done, but said he didn't feel a thing then or now. "He never showed any remorse," Ure told me. "I remember that very clearly."

Brian Clements, Nosanchuk's co-counsel for the defence, later gave his impression of Lamb to a reporter: "As a defence attorney I had a lot of interaction with Lamb, but I have to say, whenever I looked into Matthew Lamb's eyes, it was like there was no one behind them. I always felt like I was talking to the Bionic Man."

***

The next four psychiatric witnesses to testify for the defence were Dr George Darby, Dr Elliott T. Barker, Dr Barry Boyd, and psychologist Elizabeth Willet who had together made the long trek from the Oak Ridge Facility for the Criminally Insane at Penetanguishene to Windsor for Lamb's trial. These four doctors had examined Lamb in summer 1966 before declaring him sane and capable of participating in his own defence. Despite this, Nosanchuk needed their clinical opinions regarding Lamb's inability to fully appreciate the consequences of his killing spree due to his "psychopathic" personality.

Dr George Darby, clinical director of Oak Ridge, was the first of four Penetanguishene psychiatrists to testify. What Darby told the court shocked Nosanchuk—who likely wished he hadn't asked the doctor to take the stand. Turning to the jury, Darby recounted how he found Lamb to be a consummate liar, whose statements should not be believed under any circumstances. Lamb had "repeatedly lied to him" and "changed his story three times regarding his role" in the shootings. The psychiatrist diagnosed Lamb as antisocial and hostile with a psychopathic personality.

Nosanchuk realized his high-profile defence witness was, as he later wrote, "making the prosecution's case," but partially salvaged this potential catastrophe by falling back on the psychopath's inability to feel remorse. With a careful line of questioning, Nosanchuk managed to get Darby to state that while Lamb intellectually knew what he was doing on June 25, he "was incapable of foreseeing the full consequences of his actions or perceiving their 'full force' on an emotional level." Thankfully for the defence, three other expert witnesses were still to take the stand.

Unknown at the time of Lamb's murder trial, Dr Barry Boyd and Dr Elliott T. Barker had an ulterior motive in testifying for the defence. Both men wanted Lamb committed at their Oak Ridge Facility, as Lamb was a promising candidate for a highly experimental and controversial therapy program. Young and highly intelligent psychopathic men like Lamb were believed most likely to benefit from—and hopefully prove—the efficacy of their experiment.

Barker testified how Lamb admitted he viewed everyone like "bugs" except "maybe his grandmother and a favourite uncle." Justice Stark interrupted Barker's testimony to ask the witness if Lamb could comprehend the terrible crime he committed. "Emotionally, Lamb considered his killings the same way you or I might view swatting a fly," Barker explained, and the judge seemed satisfied with the analogy. Barker concluded his testimony by theorizing Lamb's stunted emotional development rendered him incapable of appreciating the full significance of the act of killing two human beings. Interestingly, he specifically mentioned that Lamb was not suffering from psychosis on the night of his shooting spree—contradicting the testimony of Drs Yaworsky, Dolan, and Scott.

Dr Barry Boyd, superintendent of Oak Ridge, repeated the opinions voiced by his program director, Dr Barker. Boyd testified Lamb told him during an interview six months prior to the trial: "I hate everybody on the street and I will probably kill someone else before I die—it doesn't bother me at all. It's like stepping on a bug."

In his cross-examination, Duchesne extracted admissions from both Boyd and Barker that Lamb was cognitively aware of his actions with an absence of psychosis during the shooting spree, although both psychiatrists stubbornly maintained Lamb's "emotional immaturity" hindered his ability to fully appreciate the significance of his actions. Duchesne did his best to exploit the divergent opinions and contradictions in the defence's expert testimony, but neither doctor fully took the bait.

Dr Elizabeth Willet, a psychologist at the Penetanguishene facility, was the last medical witness to testify for the defence. She told the court Lamb's intelligence tested in the ninety-third percentile with an IQ of 126, but further tests showed Lamb's emotional development was equivalent to that of a three-to-six-year-old child. Willet diagnosed Lamb as having low impulse control, a high rate of aggression, and low frustration tolerance, stating, "Lamb intellectually understood society's sanctions and the responsibilities expected of his own behaviour," but that they had little effect on him. She argued that Lamb showed "sadistic proclivities" and would do whatever was necessary to gratify his immediate desires. "Subconsciously, I must feel something," he told her in interview, "but when I pull the trigger I feel nothing.

It's like shooting off a cap gun." Interestingly, Willet said Lamb was not living in a fantasy world—directly contradicting Dr Scott of Kingston Penitentiary—but that he lacked the "empathetic brake" that affects one's decision to truly appreciate the consequences of one's violent acts. As such, Willett concluded Lamb was someone suffering from "episodic psychopathy."

As the final witness for the defence, Nosanchuk called Constable Donald Graham of the former Riverside Police Department to the stand. Graham told the court how in February 1964, he had been working off hours as a security officer at the Riverside Arena when physically assaulted by Lamb in an unprovoked attack. He detailed the various weapons found on Lamb, and that it was the first time that the troubled youth, then sixteen years old, came to the attention of the legal system. Lamb served six months in a juvenile correctional facility near London, Ontario, for the assault. This may seem to be a bold move—showing a pattern of violence—but Nosanchuk was chancing that Graham's testimony depicted Lamb as an unpredictable, violent psychopath whose crimes lacked reason or motive—reinforcing his contention that Lamb was insane when he shot four strangers. His gamble paid off. The prosecution did not see the opportunity that Nosanchuk had created for them—which could have been a serious error on the part of the defence. By the defence bringing up Lamb's past crimes, Duchesne could have taken advantage and opened the floodgates to examine Lamb's history of violence. Furthermore, the prosecution chose not to challenge the defence's "absence of motive" logic for the assault.

Following Constable Graham's testimony, defence attorneys Nosanchuk and Clements rested their case for the defence. There is no doubt Lamb received a first-rate defence. The team's tracking down of witnesses from Lamb's earliest years and cajoling seven medical professionals to travel hundreds of kilometres to testify was the result of thorough pretrial preparatory work on Lamb's behalf. Further, the defence's courtroom performance was near flawless, a fact even more impressive considering Lamb was a destitute legal aid case that Nosanchuk took on pro bono. They painted a vivid picture for the jury that traversed the spectrum of abnormal behaviour: from Lamb as living in a dream world since childhood, starring in his personal cowboy movie the night of his killing spree; to an insane man-child suffering from "amnesia" while trapped in a temporary "psychotic episode"; to a violent, deceptive psychopath and manipulative liar willing to say anything or tell any story, no matter how implausible, to avoid taking responsibility for his horrific crimes. Although the defence's medical opinions differed substantially, all unanimously insisted Lamb's psychopathic personality limited his ability to "fully appreciate" the consequences of his shooting rampage. Would this point of consensus be enough to convince a jury? Would they see Lamb's lack of remorse or guilt for his crime as equivalent to failing to understand his crimes or know they were wrong? Would the jury determine Lamb's personality disorder sufficiently debilitating to acquit him on grounds of insanity and spare him the hangman's rope? The answer now lay within the competent hands of Duchesne and his prosecution team, who had the opportunity to bring out two last witnesses to make the case for the Crown.

***

Crown Attorney Eugene Duchesne had promised in his opening statement to present a very different Matthew Lamb to the court: a psychopath who had acted with "intent" when he gunned down four innocent strangers, knowing what he did was wrong yet contemptuous of the consequences. It was this Lamb the jury must see in order to pass a guilty verdict.

Duchesne called Dr Basil Orchard from the Oak Ridge Facility as his first psychiatric witness for the prosecution. Orchard told the court he examined Lamb the previous August, stating that the defendant first pleaded amnesia, but eventually admitted that it wasn't true. Lamb "saw no point in keeping up the pretense of not remembering what he had done once the second victim [Woloch] had died." Orchard found no symptoms of mental illness in Lamb—just a young man with strong impulses which he could usually control, but who would sometimes relieve his rage by striking out. The doctor stated with certainty that Lamb "was capable of appreciating the nature and consequences of his crime," and knew his shooting rampage on the night of June 25, 1966, to be wrong.

"You differ with every doctor we've heard from," remarked Justice Stark. There's no record of Orchard's or Duchesne's response—were they left speechless? The unlikely interruption was carefully documented by the *Star* reporter in the room, signalling that the judge's words had impact. Regardless, Orchard concluded his testimony by looking directly at the jury and issuing a prescient warning: "Finding this defendant insane would open the floodgates for psychopaths everywhere to claim insanity for their own violent crimes."

Duchesne's second expert witness was Dr Wilfred Boothroyd, Associate Professor of Psychiatry and Head of Psychiatric Services at Sunnybrook Hospital in Toronto. Boothroyd was a preeminent forensic psychiatrist who testified Lamb had acted out of strong emotions of hatred and bitterness toward others. It was Boothroyd's opinion that Lamb wanted to hurt somebody, and "was aware and fully intended the consequences of the act." He conceded Lamb was probably mentally ill when placed in the prison hospital at Kingston Penitentiary in March 1966, following his release from solitary confinement, and was perhaps even in "a state of euphoric mental illness" two days after the Ford Boulevard shootings. On the night of June 25, however, "Lamb was definitely not insane." The doctor made the distinction clear: Lamb may have a psychopathic personality disorder, but he was not suffering a mental illness. Boothroyd believed that Lamb was capable of the "gamut of feeling—except guilt or conscience."

Boothroyd was interrupted in mid-sentence, just as Orchard before him had been.

"You're making a diagnosis, doctor?" Justice Stark asked.

"Yes," Boothroyd replied.

"Without seeing or examining the patient?" pressed Justice Stark. Again, Boothroyd replied affirmatively.

The justice paused. "I see," he said. Another Crown witness, another interruption—a highly unusual state of affairs. Did this impact the jury?

In the *Windsor Star,* the reporter again records this exchange, but this time, adds extra detail. The newspaper reads: "Dr Boothroyd had made it plain when he took the witness box that he had not interviewed Lamb and denied being offered the chance, although defence lawyer Saul Nosanchuk claimed to have made such an offer earlier this week." Boothroyd had based his clinical opinion on police reports, details of Lamb's personal and criminal history, and pretrial psychiatric reports of other doctors who had interviewed Lamb.

In courtrooms everywhere, jurors are purposely affected by the decorum of a courtroom; the elevated bench designed to project an aura of authority and assumed wisdom in the presiding judge. The jury would have instinctively looked to Justice Stark for guidance and clarity, placing great weight on his opinion and courtroom attitude toward witnesses when it came time to decide on a verdict. Whether from ignorance or design, Stark cast a shadow of doubt over the validity of both prosecution witnesses.

***

The time had come for final arguments. Surprisingly, Saul Nosanchuk was first to face the all-male jury and make his case for the defence. It was "crime without context," he declared, depicting Lamb's killing spree as nothing more than a senseless and bizarre act without motive. He carefully expressed the defence's utmost compassion and sympathy for the families of the deceased, and deftly tied in Lamb's neglected and loveless childhood. He reminded the jury that even if they acquitted the defendant, he would not be a free man, but "held in strict custody in a secure hospital for the criminally insane...and could be for the rest of his life."

Anticipating jurors would individually decide—despite the barrage of (albeit conflicting) psychiatric testimonies—that there just had to be something wrong with Lamb to commit such a horrendous and inexplicable act, Nosanchuk boldly urged them to simply consider Lamb's action as sufficient proof of his obvious mental illness over the weight of psychiatric testimonies. He reminded the jury how Lamb, after shooting four strangers, "then knocked on the door of a nearby home, threatening to kill Mrs Heaton and then just left without anything happening." He left the gun in a nearby field where it would be found—and went to bed as if nothing had happened. Nosanchuk cried that this act "screams out to each and every juror using common sense that here was a young teenager...who was 'insane' at the time of the shootings." With that, Nosanchuk turned and walked confidently back to the defence table, sat down, and hid his shaking hands under the table.

Crown Prosecutor Duchesne faced the jury next. He started with a starkly different version of events. "This was a case of calculated and cold-blooded murder of innocent young people walking to a bus stop in their own neighbourhood, ambushed by an ex-convict released from a federal penitentiary just three weeks before the shootings." Also appealing to the jury's common sense, Duchesne declared that it should be "a simple matter for the jury to recognize Lamb as a menace to the community" who should be held responsible for the deaths of Edith Chaykoski and Andrew Woloch. Importantly, he advised the jury that he didn't believe there was sufficient evidence to merit a conviction for capital murder as the act was not premeditated. In other words, Duchesne was telling the jury that they didn't need to send Lamb to the hangman's noose, but he could still be guilty of non-capital murder and spend his life imprisoned from society.

Duchesne argued Lamb's psychopathic personality and superior intelligence allowed him to give wildly conflicting versions of events to different psychiatrists—yet, "Lamb was still able to convince each one." He defined the defendant as a sadist "whose violent impulses needed gratification without delay"— damn the consequences. How was someone allegedly suffering from profound shock at finding himself holding a rifle in a stranger's home then able to return home and fall into a deep sleep?

Duchesne then changed tack by asking the jury to view Lamb's murder spree in a wider social context and to consider the probable ramifications should Lamb not be held accountable for his actions. The jurors were leaning forward now as Duchesne bellowed:

> Why should this type of a killer be exempted from criminal responsibility? Would not a "not guilty" verdict open the floodgates for sociopaths and psychopaths to 'beat the bushes' for psychiatrists willing to support an insanity defence in order to avoid conventional imprisonment? Would slick con artists not have a field day in striving to be classified as insane and not criminally responsible? Would not the shrewd psychopathic criminal have a much easier time in the hospital for the mentally ill than in a federal penitentiary?

Duchesne cautioned the jury that if they found Lamb not guilty by insanity, the result would provide an inexpedient precedent in Canadian law. Nosanchuk would later write how "the jurors were paying close attention to the well-reasoned arguments of the prosecutor." One newspaper reporter covering the trial also noted the rapt attention of the jury, stating in his article how jurors would "certainly return a 'guilty' verdict."

***

The final word in a Canadian criminal trial is given by the presiding judge. Justice Stark spent ninety minutes detailing the charges to the jury, explaining that they had several verdicts to choose from: guilty or not guilty of capital murder, non-capital murder, or manslaughter; or not guilty of non-capital murder by reason of insanity. Stark turned to the jurors and said he had personally reviewed the evidence and that the weight of medical evidence dictated the jury must find for the defence. He went as far as to say, "If he had no mind, it would be barbarous to convict him." Allowing this diktat to sink in, Stark then added the caveat, "However... it was up to them to decide." Seldom has a capital-murder trial jury been so clearly instructed to return a specific verdict as in the Lamb trial.

The jurors began their deliberations at 4:30 p.m. on Friday, January 20, 1967. Less than three hours later, they returned a verdict. Stark asked the defendant to rise and, standing alongside his two defence counsels, Lamb showed no reaction when the jury foreman stood up and informed the court that Lamb was "not guilty by reason of insanity." As Detective Sergeant Jim Ure escorted Lamb back to his holding cell to await a transfer to the Oak Ridge Facility, any dark images of the dreaded spectre of a rope hanging on a wooden crossbeam that had been dancing in Lamb's head faded to black, forever.

***

So how did the defence triumph over the Crown prosecutor's team? Every criminal investigator knows that just because a person acts crazy doesn't mean they don't know what they're doing, but the general public does not. That was certainly true in 1967, before television and internet docudramas gave us a rudimentary understanding of the violent psychopathic mind. Nosanchuk won an acquittal for two main reasons: As convoluted as the trial's psychiatric testimony was, the expert witnesses testifying for the defence outnumbered the prosecution's psychiatrists by a seven-to-two margin. Duchesne didn't follow the "golden rule" on how to win insanity pleas—that it is the quantity of probability that counts.

When I interviewed Nosanchuk, I asked if he won an acquittal by simply outworking Duchesne. Nosanchuk, struggling to raise his trembling right hand from beneath the hospital bedsheet covering him, shook this writer's hand, flashed that sly smile of his, and again whispered, "You said that, I didn't."

The prosecutor's failure to match Nonsanchuk's preparatory investigative work is apparent in his opening statement. Duchesne told the court of Lamb having "hid his gun" after his killing spree, yet Duchesne never took this any further. Sergeant Frank Chauvin remained, nearly fifty years later, angry and baffled, wondering why Duchesne failed to call him or his officers as trial witnesses to testify how Lamb's shotgun was found in an improvised sniper's nest behind the Heaton home—proving Lamb was mission-oriented and sane.

The prosecutorial files for Lamb's murder trial are today held in the Archives of Ontario in Toronto. Duchesne's files are not accessible to researchers or the general public due to privacy concerns. Nevertheless, the chief archivist kindly agreed to verify whether Sergeant Frank Chauvin's report detailing how Lamb's murder weapon was found was in Duchesne's prosecution files used in the trial. It was not.

So what happened to it? The report was likely lost among the massive amount of information accumulated in a murder case of this magnitude. To be gracious, Lamb's killing spree occurred during a period of unprecedented restructuring by a Windsor Police Department still coping with the administrative nightmare of absorbing five previously independent police forces after amalgamation in January 1966. Rank-and-file police officers at the time of the shooting all knew of the sniper's nest found behind the Heaton home, but the details did not clearly make their way to the witness box. Whatever exactly happened to the report, Duchesne and his research assistants failed to fully investigate, or fully appreciate, how the murder weapon was found by police in the early-morning hours of June 26, 1966. On seemingly minor details are such major issues often decided.

The second key reason for Lamb's acquittal had nothing to do with the trial proceedings. By 1967, the counterculture was questioning the efficacy of existing cultural and state institutions. The legal system was not unaffected. Rehabilitation was in the air, embedding itself in the justice system as a humane alternative to long prison terms or capital punishment.

***

The acts of Matthew Charles Lamb terminated the lives of two young adults and inflicted serious wounds on two others, leaving permanent emotional scars on victims and families alike. The Chaykoskis would be forever traumatized by the shotgun killings, afflicted with "victim's fear," a common post-traumatic neurosis that Lamb would one day be released to torment their family yet again. Windsor residents took comfort in Lamb's acquittal on grounds of insanity, convinced this dangerous young man would spend the rest of his life in maximum security behind the secure walls of the Oak Ridge Facility for the Criminally Insane and, over time, would be forgotten. In most circumstances, they would have been right. But Lamb would find a way to defy this fate. Upon arrival at Oak Ridge, he began a ten-year odyssey one newspaper columnist would later describe as A STORY TOO UNBELIEVABLE FOR FICTION.

CHAPTER NINE:

The Inmates Are Running the Asylum

OAK RIDGE WAS A BLEAK, ONE-STOREY REDBRICK fortress that first opened its doors to Ontario's most violent, mentally ill criminals on February 21, 1933. Its large, battleship-grey iron doors and barred windows gave it a frightful appearance in stark contrast to the well-kept Edwardian homes built on and around the hospital property. First occupied by Governor John Simcoe and his top commanders following the War of 1812, the 380-acre site of Oak Ridge was a naval and military base built to keep a wary eye on American ships plying the waters of Lake Huron. Situated on the southeastern tip of picturesque Georgian Bay, the Oak Ridge Facility for the Criminally Insane was a division of the Mental Health Centre at Penetanguishene—the only mental health facility of its kind in Canada.

The first four wards were constructed in 1933, and by 1956, four additional dormitories were needed to accommodate the growing number of patients sent there by the courts, penitentiaries, county jails, and other psychiatric hospitals throughout Ontario. At its peak, Oak Ridge filled three hundred beds with patients judged too mentally ill or dangerous to be incarcerated elsewhere. In 2014, almost a century after housing and treating Ontario's most dangerous criminally insane patients, Oak Ridge closed its doors for the last time and was, without fanfare, demolished. The stories of what happened there, however, would not remain buried.

***

In the early 1960s, the emerging counterculture pried open the iron gates of Oak Ridge, bringing with it an innate skepticism for all existing institutions, and demands for change. Dr Elliott T. Barker was one of four psychiatrists hired by Program Director Dr Barry Boyd and was a reformer at heart. Dr Boyd had known Dr Barker since childhood, and also knew of his interest in Social Therapy Units (STUs) and new concepts such as "therapeutic communities" for treating the criminally insane. Boyd himself had established a ward structure where patients could be voted into a "Council of 12" by their peers. Meeting biweekly, the council discussed ward policies and made recommendations, though power still ultimately lay with the medical staff.

Barker arrived at Oak Ridge in 1965 as the new director of social therapy. He immediately discarded Oak Ridge's traditional reliance on tranquilizers and electroconvulsive therapy (ECT) to control patients, introducing instead something Barker called "compulsive community therapy." The resulting STU opened that September, and would soon grow to occupy half of the wards. Together, Barker and Boyd set out to create a "new" Oak Ridge, based on a radical new idea: psychopathy could be cured.

Barker believed that psychopathy and schizophrenia were mental illnesses rooted in the patient's inability to communicate and interact with others; that beneath a thin veneer of normalcy lay a deep-rooted psychosis from which these mental disorders originated. Barker's goal was to expose this "hidden psychosis," treat it, and eliminate it—thereby curing the patient and returning them to sanity.

Dr Barker first organized all three hundred mentally ill inmates at Oak Ridge into small groups based on similarity of diagnoses and abilities, with each group represented by patient-run ward committees. Barker, however, set his sights on G Ward, which consisted of thirty-eight patients evenly split between violent psychopaths and schizophrenics with average to above average intelligence. These patients would be required to undertake a chemically induced journey of self-discovery in search of their "hidden psychosis," while simultaneously learning to take responsibility for their crimes—necessary antecedents for curing them of psychopathy. Drs Boyd and Barker were familiar with Lamb's criminal history, high intelligence quotient, and psychopathic personality. They immediately assigned Lamb to the G Ward alongside previously chosen inmates—with murderers, attempted murderers, and serial rapists.

Barker's STU program was inspired by British psychiatrist Maxwell Jones's pioneer work developing "therapeutic communities" and STU programs at Belmont Hospital in London, England. The STU at Oak Ridge developed into a multi-stage program, designed to work in tandem within the patient-run "therapeutic community." Patients started in the H Ward and progressed through to the G, F, and finally E Ward. The G and F Wards were the most psychotherapeutic in nature. In 1966, only one year after Barker's arrival, all STU sessions became compulsory.

The STU began in the H Ward—the beginning of the patient's indoctrination into the program's philosophy. It featured the MAP (Motivation, Attitude, and Participation) program as a form of re-education for patients. Groups of usually four to eight would sit on the bare floor for eight hours a day, totally mute, for fourteen straight days. They were not allowed to stand; only two moves per group were permitted. If patients failed or refused to comply, they were punished—either verbally, through sedation, or by being put into restraints or placed in solitary confinement.

Patients who showed promise were cherry-picked to move on to the next phase, in the G Ward. Here, Barker modified his STU program with a new therapeutic tool he named Defence-Disrupting Therapy (DDT). The program started with group therapy sessions deliberately calculated to agitate patients—often while drugged and in a state of mental confusion resulting from sleep deprivation—beyond their personal breaking points until patients admitted their mental illness and renounced their defective personalities.

The majority of these high-tension social therapy sessions were held in an enclosed area at the end of the hallway on the G Ward: a three-walled vestibule with a single barred entrance, sparsely decorated with twelve to sixteen plastic chairs aligned beneath a barred window that extended the length of one entire wall, giving the room its nickname "the sunroom." Patients sat for long periods in uncomfortable chairs during these therapy sessions, usually overseen by Barker himself or assistant "patient therapists," and quite often Barker's successor at Oak Ridge, Dr Gary Maier.

Psychedelic drugs were a crucial component of DDT starting in March 1966. Patients were injected with sodium amytal, known as the "truth serum." Since it was a sedative, doctors counteracted it with methedrine, a central nervous system stimulant. By the time Matthew Charles Lamb arrived a year later, patients on the G Ward were being dosed with LSD and methamphetamine. These consciousness-altering drugs were freely distributed upon patient request or force-fed into reluctant patients unwilling to submit to the mandatory drug regimen. In fact, patient committees developed to a point where they were involved in decisions about medication and dosing, punishment, and group assignment.

In the sunroom, patients badgered each other mercilessly, with Lamb and other true believers in Barker's methods ganging up on new arrivals or obstinate patients to make them admit their crimes and acknowledge their insanity. Emotions ran so high during these marathon therapy sessions that patients were often restrained to their chairs by leather handcuffs—an idea suggested by one of Barker's patients and subsequently adopted. Should this tactic fail to calm or "break" a patient, two security guards would quietly enter the sunroom, place themselves directly behind the upset patient, and choke him into unconsciousness with a towel. This approach left no ligature marks on the patient and often worked, at least until the session ended. If a patient was self-harming or thought to be suicidal, he would be handcuffed to a fellow patient for "safety." Patients in G Ward cynically referred to Barker's STU sessions in the sunroom as "the hundred-day hate-in."

Augmenting Barker's DDT program was the Total Encounter Capsule (TEC) on the F Ward. The TEC was a sensory-deprivation chamber measuring two by three metres with four soundproof walls and padded floor, all painted green; the ceiling was equipped with a one-way mirror, and there was a sink and a toilet. Television cameras were mounted inside two of the walls—likely one of the first times that videotape was used as a "therapeutic" tool. The mirrored ceiling and television cameras were used by fellow patients for monitoring the capsule's inhabitants around the clock. They were to note all activity inside the capsule, including conversations, any noticeable changes in patient behaviour or mood, and were specifically directed by Barker to note the dynamics of patient interactions inside the capsule. Patient monitors could also quickly enter the capsule in the event of physical fights or medical emergencies. The TEC patient's only source of sustenance while inside the capsule was water, tea, soup, or juice—often spiked with amphetamines and hallucinogens—fed through a straw by small holes drilled through the fifteen-centimetre-thick sealed door. If a patient was deemed too sullen or withdrawn from others sharing the capsule "experience," patient monitors ensured amphetamines and hallucinogenic tablets were surreptitiously administered.

Barker insisted patients enter the capsule naked, a detail that caused considerable controversy when leaked to the general public. Barker refused to yield to external pressure, telling critics "a naked person would be more inclined to reveal naked thoughts." The capsule was typically occupied by two to seven patients at any given time for periods lasting up to two weeks. That's a long time to be isolated, high on drugs, and deprived of solid food. Temperature inside the capsule was maintained at thirty-two degrees Celsius; the place was described by some patients as a "sweat box" made more uncomfortable when crowded with inmates—men further frustrated by their inability to escape the constant bright light maintained inside the capsule. Every fifteen hours the lights inside flickered momentarily, allowing outside observers to count the number of "wet tissue bombs" stuck against the sweat-drenched walls. Thrown by patients inside the capsule, each wet tissue found stuck against the opposite wall signified to observing patient monitors that an "element of trust" had been established between two patients within the TEC.

The point of the Total Encounter Capsule experience was to confirm Barker's theory that his modified capsule could facilitate, or manufacture, the necessary conditions for expressing "empathy"—a primary emotion lacking in the psychopathic mind—among the criminally insane patients living together in isolation, while individually pursuing their chemically induced search for their "hidden psychosis." As Barker succinctly put it: "The goal is to cure you, even if I must first drive you mad."

***

In the winter of 1967, shortly after Lamb's arrival on G Ward, media interest in Oak Ridge was at an all-time high, reflecting the growing public concern over Barker's experimental program. Drs Boyd and Barker decided to confront head-on the public rumours of baton-wielding guards beating terrified mental patients by inviting two Toronto *Globe and Mail* reporters to observe firsthand the STU and DDT programs in action. They would be the first of many national and international media outlets, such as

CBC, CTV, the National Film Board of Canada, and the BBC, to follow in the years to come.

The media, once allowed to observe the STU/DDT program first-hand, promoted the perceived benefits of Barker's radical approach for curing violent psychopaths and schizophrenics through various documentaries and television specials aired in the late 1960s and 1970s. The first outsider allowed to observe Barker's patient-run "therapeutic community" on G Ward was Joan Hollobon, a science editor from the *Globe and Mail* who, in 1968, wrote a complimentary article extolling her growing ability to identify with the patients and see their essential humanity. She concluded her article by asking readers: "Regardless of what triggered these men to commit such horrible crimes…have I not at times also felt like that?" After two days spent inside the capsule, another reporter wrote how he personally witnessed that elusive "empathy" when he observed one naked patient move his foot to softly caress the big toe of a fellow patient showing signs of distress while inside the capsule. A more critical reporter, following a short stint inside the capsule, wrote of frustrated and angry patients; overhearing one muttering to another as they left the capsule, "I am so sick of this shit!"

In the beginning, patient enthusiasm for Barker's STU/DDT program was generally high, as the patient-run program relieved the boredom of long-term confinement and provided a never-ending supply of popular street drugs, while empowering patients with belief in their own agency in recovering their sanity. Barker wrote numerous journal articles during this period for the Canadian Psychiatric Association, and published numerous academic papers between 1968 and 1977, promoting his STU/DDT "therapeutic community" and its objectives. Barker's final 1977 article in the *Canadian Journal of Psychiatry* on the Oak Ridge program was typically unapologetic in its provocative introduction: "For the last nine years, on a regular basis, groups of naked mental patients have been locked together in a small room for periods ranging up to eleven days." Barker claimed early in the program that 90 percent of his patients found the STU and Total Encounter Capsule experiences beneficial to their rehabilitation. Indeed, some patients expressed a desire to remain incarcerated over obtaining their freedom, arguing they preferred to complete the program before they would feel comfortable being released back into society.

Later research conducted by sociologist Richard Weisman in his objective study of Barker's STU/DDT therapeutic community found roughly half of the patients justified the deprivations they endured in Barker's program as a necessary means to a desired outcome. However, a similar number of patients constantly resisted or complained of the physical brutality and psychological trauma, arguing the STU was disguised institutionalized torture devoid of any therapeutic benefit. Responding to criticism of his coercive methods, Barker argued: "I wouldn't do that to people on the street, but for people who have already offended society to a degree they lost their liberty...I didn't mind getting a bit coercive psychologically."

Such were the conditions confronting Matthew Lamb on G Ward in the winter of 1967. Lamb was reportedly enthusiastic from the start about Barker's experimental program, and soon established a close personal relationship both with Barker and with Oak Ridge director Dr Barry Boyd. Lamb quickly became a leader within a therapeutic community of thirty-eight violent offenders, most of whom were older than Lamb and had more seniority at Oak Ridge. In early 1969, Lamb was elected by his peers to "patient therapist." Barker justified his use of patient therapists, both to critics within and outside Oak Ridge, by arguing, "No one was better positioned to understand the criminally insane mind...than a fellow patient similarly afflicted."

In scholarly journals, Barker wrote of Lamb's leadership skills as the reason for his election to "patient therapist," but in the politicized and high-tension atmosphere where patients sought to endear themselves to Barker—an influential member of the Panel Review Board, which had the power to release patients from Oak Ridge—Lamb's promotion by his peers strongly suggests voting patients were influenced as much by Lamb's closeness to Barker than by any enthusiasm they may have harboured for Lamb himself.

As a "patient therapist," Lamb supervised STU group sessions, collected and collated data on patients being monitored in the capsule, and even wrote pharmaceutical prescriptions that Barker typically endorsed with a flick of his pen after a cursory glance. Lamb thrived in the Oak Ridge environment, living in a highly structured, safe environment where he enjoyed the respect of Drs Barker and Boyd and—for the first time in his life—the prestige of holding an official position of authority. Even so, Lamb's enthusiasm for Oak Ridge's STU/DDT program and new-found literary interest in "abnormal psychology" was not enough to dissuade Lamb from his then secret long-term goals.

When informed of Lamb's promotion to patient therapist less than two years after arriving at Oak Ridge, Lamb's arresting officer for capital murder, Windsor Police Inspector Jim Ure, had this to say on the matter:

> A grade-nine education made a therapist responsible for treating our most dangerous criminals? Well, he [Barker] would have done well in California with the rest of the kooks. I can't remember exactly, but it was a couple of years after Lamb had been sent to the insane asylum at Penetang, when reports started filtering back to us [Windsor Police] detectives of Lamb's sexual relationship with a top official at Penetang.

The validity of these allegations and rumours cannot be confirmed, but are indicative of the controversy and scandal surrounding Barker's experimental program to cure psychopaths during his tenure as the director of Social Therapy at Oak Ridge from 1965 to 1972—at least from the perspective of law enforcement.

***

Prior to the policy changes of the mid-1960s under Boyd and Barker, no murderer had ever been released from Oak Ridge. Violent offenders traditionally spent the rest of their lives on hospital grounds, a fact well-known in popular discourse where quips such as "he was sent to Penetang" implied the subject being discussed was unlikely to be seen again. Yet the full rehabilitation of habitual and violent criminals was the new operating culture at Oak Ridge in 1965, and by 1968, murderers previously judged criminally insane were being released back into society based on the recommendation of the three-member Panel Review Board—when the patient was deemed to no longer pose any risks to himself or others. This was a radical change from the historic operating culture at the maximum-security facility of Oak Ridge, yet symptomatic of the revolutionary ideals of the counterculture affecting Canada's penal system by the late 1960s. The new catch, treat, and release policy at Oak Ridge failed to live up to expectations. The case of two Oak Ridge patients incarcerated with Lamb illustrates how good intentions, but poor judgment, by Ontario's mental health authorities produced disastrous results.

Seventeen-year-old Peter Woodcock was a short, frail, and effeminate youth, five feet four and about 135 pounds when he first arrived at Oak Ridge in April 1957. An intellectually gifted young killer, Woodcock appeared incapable of harming anyone, yet is today still considered one of Canada's all-time, top-ten most brutal killers. A native of Toronto, Woodcock received national notoriety as Canada's youngest serial killer for sexually assaulting, torturing, and murdering three children—two boys and one girl between four and nine years of age—during a nine-month period in 1956–57. Apprehended and charged in early 1957, Woodcock was judged to be a psychopath and criminally insane. The Crown prosecutor for Woodcock's case agreed to the defendant's incarceration at Oak Ridge, forgoing a criminal trial, secure in the knowledge that Woodcock's fate was a guaranteed life sentence served in the maximum-security mental facility. Prosecutors of that era preferred incarceration at Oak Ridge over a trial with a guilty verdict, as Canadian law mandated convicted prisoners serving a life sentence had to be unconditionally released after thirty years. Remember, Oak Ridge, up to that time, had never released a murderer. By 1969, however, the opposite was true, and Canadian prosecutors now fought for prison terms, assuming offenders sentenced to mental health facilities had a quick ticket to freedom.

In 1968, Woodcock was enrolled with Lamb in Barker's STU and DDT program. Having already served ten years at Oak Ridge, Woodcock had a good understanding of the social dynamics of life there and knew how best to exploit them for his personal benefit. Woodcock ingratiated himself with his fellow patients, but was apparently disliked and distrusted by his peers—primarily due to his incessant sexual stalking of them. Throughout the facility, Woodcock was resented by other patients competing for the sexual attentions of the more attractive patients and new arrivals to Oak Ridge. Hospital records report Woodcock routinely sent anonymous, threatening letters to inmates who dared interfere with his manic pursuit of sexually desirable patients. He routinely manipulated, blackmailed, and threatened vulnerable patients into granting him sexual favours. Barker realized Woodcock's sexual fantasies were too strong to overcome, so Woodcock was removed from G Ward and was inexplicably transferred to the minimum-security mental hospital at Brockville, Ontario. There, Woodcock was indulged with visits to train museums—trains and streetcars had always fascinated him. He was even allowed to go to the movies to see *The Silence of the Lambs*, an Oscar-winning film about serial killers that Woodcock reportedly enjoyed.

With psychiatrists reporting real progress, Woodcock was eventually given his first unescorted day pass, and allowed to leave Brockville Mental Health Centre in the company of former Brockville mental patient Bruce Hamill, a murderer and former lover of Woodcock when both men were incarcerated at Oak Ridge.

Hamill and Woodcock immediately carried out their pre-planned murder of Dennis Kerr, another inmate at Brockville who had rejected Woodcock's sexual advances. Within an hour of Woodcock's release on his first day pass, he and Hamill enticed inmate Kerr over to a wooded area on the periphery of the Brockville hospital grounds on the pretext of paying Kerr money Woodcock owed him. Kerr was repeatedly beaten, stabbed, anally raped, disemboweled, and almost decapitated during a two-hour sado-sexual frenzy. After raping and further mutilating Kerr's body post-mortem, Woodcock—drenched in Kerr's blood— walked three kilometres to a police station and turned himself in. Woodcock reportedly commented to the arresting officer, "What a shame. This is such a tragedy; such a tragedy."

Both men were once again found not guilty by reason of insanity and incarcerated in separate mental hospitals. Hamill was again incarcerated at Brockville Mental Health Centre while Woodcock was returned to Oak Ridge, where he resided until his death in 2010. Peter Woodcock's sentence as a psychopathic pedophile serial killer—which began and ended in the maximum-security facility at Oak Ridge—was an indictment of the often naive and subjective nature of psychiatric diagnoses of the era, operating within a bumbling mental-health-care bureaucracy— which when combined allowed such a travesty to occur.

Dr Elliott T. Barker's reputed talent for identifying psychopaths while employed at Oak Ridge also appeared to be overrated. Participants in Barker's STU/DDT program had, for the most part, been sent to Oak Ridge for committing the worst of crimes while supposedly in a state of legal insanity—but there were exceptions. Steve Smith had never been charged or convicted of a serious crime, yet found himself living a nightmare when sent to Oak Ridge in 1968 and locked up alongside Ontario's most brutal and dangerous criminals. Smith, a fellow patient with Lamb at Oak Ridge, following his release from custody, wrote a memoir called *The Psychopath Machine* recounting his experiences as a misdiagnosed psychopath placed in Barker's STU/DDT program.

Events leading up to Steve Smith's incarceration at Oak Ridge are instructive. Smith's unlikely odyssey into the world of the criminally insane began in the late winter of 1968. Like many teenagers of the counterculture, Smith sought to escape the emotional and physical abuse of the dysfunctional home he shared with his brother, mother, and her alcoholic lover in Sault Ste. Marie, Ontario. Other than a few minor brushes with the Sault Ste. Marie Police while still a juvenile, Smith had no past history of violence or a criminal record. In early April 1968, he and a local friend were seized by the wanderlust that beckons the young, deciding to hitchhike to the West Coast, a favoured destination of Canadian teenagers during the turbulent 1960s and early 1970s. With little planning or foresight, Smith and his friend set out hitchhiking westward in freezing winter temperatures along Lake Superior, only to find themselves stranded in White River, Ontario—what Steve calls the "coldest town in Canada"—two days later. With no money, the stores all closed, and without shelter in the mind-numbing cold, they stole a car from a small used-car lot. Reaching the next town just before dawn, the two young men were stopped by police while in the process of abandoning the stolen car at a local service station. When arrested, Smith admits he was carrying two tablets of "acid" (LSD)—the choice drug of the counterculture, which he had planned to save until Vancouver to celebrate reaching their destination. After he had quickly swallowed both LSD tablets to avoid being charged with possession of illegal drugs in addition to stealing a car, Steve's memories of the next twenty-four hours were "a series of mental snapshots...of being violently ill at a hospital...and lying handcuffed on the cold floor in a jail cell." In his first court appearance the day after his arrest and still hallucinating from the LSD, Smith recalls "standing in a courtroom full of 'skeletons in black robes'." The presiding judge noted Steve Smith's drugged condition and sent him to the local psychiatric hospital for thirty days of observation.

"The hospital interviewed me one or two times...returned my street clothes and allowed me to wander the hospital grounds unattended. Had I wanted to, I could have easily walked away on more than one occasion," Steve said. One day, a girl from another ward invited Smith to accompany her to a dance on hospital grounds. Walking to the dance, Smith was stopped by a hospital attendant who objected to his "hippie" attire, which consisted of bell-bottom jeans, bead necklace, and headband—the typical teen attire of the late 1960s. Smith claims the attendant became hostile when he protested, pushing Smith against the wall and pawing at his jeans, while muttering something about "improper dress." Smith instinctively fought back, an act he would come to deeply regret. Dragged away by hospital staff, Smith was stripped naked, drugged, and thrown into a small cell. The hospital's clinical record of this incident, dated April 26, 1968, states: "Steve Smith tends to become resentful, hostile and uncooperative when he is not able to get his own way."

When informed he would be transferred to Penetanguishene's Oak Ridge the following day, Smith was overcome with fear, for Oak Ridge had a widespread, notorious reputation for incarcerating people who were never seen again. Young people everywhere commonly referred to people acting in a violent or crazed manner as "Penetang material."

Smith was bundled onto a train, handcuffed, and with two burly guards as escorts, arrived at the Oak Ridge Facility where he languished in a cell for days. Despite Smith's pleading with men passing by his cell wearing street clothes and conversing like doctors, his questions regarding his situation were ignored. The lack of personal contact, and eating from paper plates and plastic spoons slipped through a small door in his cell, only added to his fear and paranoia. Smith's first contact with Oak Ridge officials was a demand that Smith take an IQ test. Shortly after, Dr Barker entered Smith's cell—friendly, smiling, benevolent. Placing his arm around Steve's shoulder, Barker asked Smith if he felt he was mentally ill. Replying that he thought he wasn't, Smith listened in astonishment as Barker explained that he, Smith, was "a very sick boy, a very slick psychopath now in a facility with men just like him, some who have been locked up for over twenty years."

Terrified by Barker's implied threat of being locked up for years, Smith was offered "an opportunity for eventual release" from Oak Ridge if he volunteered for Barker's treatment program. Desperate, Smith agreed to cooperate.

Released from his cell, Smith showered, put on fresh clothes, and was immediately taken to the sunroom on G Ward, where a session of group therapy was in progress. Barker told Smith he was locking him in with six or seven inmates, all approximately the same age as Smith, to "shake things up a bit." The inmates, who had all been there for a week or more, badgered and bullied him to admit he was mentally ill. Smith's resistance and unwillingness to concede the point—believing his sanity was the one thing he was sure of—only intensified the psychological abuse from his fellow inmates. After a few days, patients decided Smith needed something to "open him up," and requested methamphetamine as a "conversational stimulant," which was subsequently approved by Barker. Smith was force-fed a cocktail of drugs designed to break his resistance and help reveal his "hidden psychosis," the seminal event from Smith's past that Barker believed could unlock the mystery of Smith's alleged psychopathy.

According to Smith, Barker "drove men into a drug-induced psychosis in an environment of fear and discipline, regulated and enforced by the patients themselves under Barker's close supervision, creating a self-sustaining system of docile mental patients." Smith witnessed and experienced the methods of coercion used at Oak Ridge, including using a twisted towel to choke patients into unconsciousness—a procedure Smith himself endured a number of times before coming to the realization that submitting to the drug regimen was preferable to the "towel treatment." Smith's submission led to his assignment as an "observer," requiring he stay awake all night to monitor and document the sleep patterns of fellow patients. To remain awake, Smith was given all the Benzedrine and amphetamines he wanted.

After a few nights of drugged sleep deprivation, he started hallucinating that bugs were crawling on his skin. Frightened

at the sight, Smith showed fellow patients and hospital attendants his arm and the non-existent "bugs" tormenting him. The
patient therapists found this highly amusing, and shortly after,
hospital attendants, without a word of explanation, placed Smith
in handcuffs and leg restraints. Left on a mattress on the cold
floor, Smith started suffering "full-blown psychotic paranoia,"
seeing bugs and worms crawling all over the floor. Believing the
two patients locked in the cell with him were conspiring to hurt
him, Smith attacked the two men. The regimen of hallucinogenic
drugs and sleep deprivation caused the violent outburst and,
from Smith's perspective, was the excuse Barker needed to introduce him to Defence-Disrupting Therapy." He was first given a
series of injections of that "truth serum" scopolamine, used in
Nazi Germany for interrogation purposes. Its effects include
dehydration, severe swelling of the throat, and constricted
breathing, resulting in an elevated pulse rate and a sense of suffo-
cation and extreme anxiety in the patient. High on scopolamine
and amphetamines, Smith was—together with other "problem
patients" in Barker's program—handcuffed to two other patients
who would ensure the drug-injected patients did not bash their
head into the walls or hyperventilate to a point where their life
was threatened.

Smith found some comfort when he was befriended by a
physically unimpressive, innocent-looking patient who, intrigued
by Smith's "hippie" persona, wanted to know all about the radical lifestyle of the counterculture. After all, Peter Woodcock had
been incarcerated in Oak Ridge since 1957. Smith was amused
by Woodcock's attempts to copy his style of dress and letting his
own hair grow long. When Woodcock later confided in Smith
the intimate details of his child murders, Smith made an effort
to mollify the friendship, stating he "still has nightmares from
that conversation." Smith had never done real "jail time" before
Oak Ridge and made it clear to Woodcock he was a heterosexual
uninterested in changing. Smith was saved from his little friend's

jealous wrath when Woodcock became infatuated with another patient. All these events took place within the first two weeks of Smith's arrival at Oak Ridge.

Smith does not recall much of the following months spent in a drug-soaked existence punctuated with extreme brutality at the hands of patient therapists and hospital staff attendants. One of only two names of the patient therapists Smith clearly recalls today is that of Matthew Charles Lamb. Given Lamb's position of authority over other inmates and reputation as an enforcer for Drs Boyd and Barker's "therapeutic community," it is not surprising Smith recalls the name of Oak Ridge's "golden boy."

Fortunately for Smith, public pressure surrounding the controversial goings-on at Oak Ridge led to the creation in 1968 of a new Patient Review Board, which allowed inmates at Oak Ridge the opportunity to appeal their incarceration. Smith immediately applied for a meeting with the Review Board. In less than half an hour, the Review Board agreed there was no evidence of "violence without cause" in Smith's past—plus, the car-theft charge had been dropped seven months earlier. Smith was told he would be unconditionally released from custody pending submission of the board's decision. Smith's misdiagnosis by Dr Barker as a dangerous psychopath eight months earlier was over.

Steve Smith left Oak Ridge in late 1968 a broken man, psychologically and spiritually. Prior to his arrest and incarceration, Smith had, like most teenagers of the counterculture, periodically tried recreational drugs. He had tried LSD just once prior to his arrest, but having been kept on a steady diet of amphetamines and hallucinogens throughout his eight months at Oak Ridge, he emerged a full-blown junkie addicted to amphetamines. Through a series of events Smith found his way back into Oak Ridge. This time, Dr Barker told him that he was there for a thirty-day assessment, which would decide whether he was to stay there in the program or go to Kingston Penitentiary. This time, however, Smith was to play a new role: teacher.

Smith was placed in a group of newcomers to the program in the H Ward, but he was wearing street clothes. "I knew they didn't understand I was also a prisoner," he writes. Someone else entered the room, arms full of papers. It was Matthew Charles Lamb.

Here's how Smith describes him:

> Lamb, on the other hand, was awe-inspiring [...] articulate, handsome, and charming. He was a natural leader. Given the opportunity, I'm sure he could have had a successful and productive life. But here he was, the leader of the pack. All crazies. [...] I will never be able to associate the Matt Lamb I knew with the psychopath who shot four people. I have no doubt that Lamb was a psychopath, but, excuse me, he was a beautiful psychopath. He was a perfect psychopath. Perhaps groomed from birth.

Smith joined Lamb and two other patient teachers in running the ward, conducting brainwashing exercises, similar to the Milgram experiment at Yale University. He was also forced to monitor patient activities in the Compressed Encounter Therapy Unit. At the end of his thirty days, Smith was sent off to Kingston Penitentiary, before bouncing around to other prisons until he was released.

Living in a car, homeless, with an arm riddled with needle tracks, Smith fought his way back to sobriety and a normal life. He would never forget what happened to him in the "psychopath machine" or the Matthew Lamb he met there.

***

It was sometime in 1970—three years into Lamb's six-year incarceration at Oak Ridge—that Roger Hammond, an old childhood friend of Lamb's, made an unexpected visit to Penetanguishene.

Hammond, a paramedic at that time, was returning a prisoner to Oak Ridge when it suddenly dawned on him that Lamb was incarcerated there. He had not seen or spoken to Lamb since the break-in and shootout at Lakeview Marine six years earlier:

> Like I said, I always liked Matt [Lamb] and I don't
> think I'd seen him since that Christmas Eve break-in
> at Lakeview Marine way back in 1964 [...] I wasn't in
> Windsor when Lamb did those Ford Boulevard killings
> [...] Anyway, I decided to pay Lamb a visit after drop-
> ping off my prisoner. Well, let me tell you, you'd have
> to see this place. I've been in the worst dungeons they
> called jails and the worst of Ontario's mental hospitals,
> but nothing quite prepared me for Oak Ridge. Just the
> looks you would get from guys sweeping the floors sent
> shivers down your back.

Hammond asked the security desk for an audience with Lamb and was politely directed by the on-shift security officer to the cafeteria located on the basement floor. "He [Lamb] is usually down in the kitchen around this time of day. Don't worry, you'll find him," the guard told Hammond. "Lamb immediately recog- nized me with a big smile on his face and ran over to give me a hug after all those years." Hammond had a little time to spare and readily accepted Lamb's invitation to stay for lunch. As they slowly made their way through the buffet line in the cafeteria, every time Lamb grabbed something from a hot tray, he looked over at Hammond, smiling and shaking his head, obviously thrilled with the surprise visit. Motioning his guest to a nearby chair, Lamb excitedly whispered to Hammond:

> "I'm getting out of here soon."
> "What, you're going to escape?"
> "No, no, I'm going to be a mercenary."

Somewhat taken aback, Hammond made an off-colour joke about this choice of profession being something Lamb would likely be good at—plus he'd be getting paid for it:

> Lamb laughed with that same evil sneering laugh I
> never liked. I couldn't believe it! I took Lamb's bragging
> about his future mercenary life in stride, as typical
> Lamb bullshit… he was always a smooth talker that
> could talk your pants off you if you didn't know him
> well. I figured he was just blowing smoke up my ass
> again. I wished him well and said goodbye as I needed
> to get back to Windsor. I never gave it a second thought
> until years later. Whoa boy!

Little did Hammond know just where his troubled childhood friend would end up.

***

Dr Elliott T. Barker unexpectedly resigned his position as director of Social Therapy at Oak Ridge in late 1972, surprising Oak Ridge staff and residents alike. Barker told his disappointed superior and lifelong friend, Dr Barry Boyd, of his growing discomfort with the conservative "winds of change" blowing through the Ontario Mental Health Centre, with the government determined to "tighten up" policy and procedures at Oak Ridge and other provincially funded mental hospitals. The great societal backlash of the early 1970s against the excesses of the 1960s counterculture had come home to roost atop the steel-grey doors at Oak Ridge.

While Barker's program was still regarded by the psychiatric profession and media as groundbreaking, the doctor nevertheless foresaw political difficulties and chose to retire to his nearby two-hundred-acre farm while remaining an unpaid mentor to his protege and successor, Dr Gary Maier. Before leaving Oak Ridge in late 1972, Barker took Dr Maier aside, warning him: "The times are changing here [Oak Ridge], so you've got to be on your guard." Unfortunately, future events suggest Maier failed to heed Barker's warning. A true believer in Barker's STU/DDT program, Maier was determined to take the Oak Ridge program "to a new level."

Maier met with his mentor on a weekly basis at Barker's farmhouse to discuss the ongoing program and fondly recounts these night sessions at Barker's home: "On Wednesday nights, I would go to Barker's farm...we would talk about issues and I found it exciting. I got to know him in his own setting...one night while we talked a chicken sat on his head!"

Maier's appointment as Barker's replacement would prove to be a disastrous choice. Unlike the charismatic and politically astute Barker, Maier was more of a "free spirit" who preferred a less regulated environment. He dramatically increased the use of LSD, sodium amytal, and scopolamine, while placing too many patients on hallucinogens and amphetamines at any given time—a process hospital staff considered a careless security risk. Maier also introduced new ideas such as Zen Buddhism and Yoga techniques to patients on G Ward, insisting all chairs be removed from the sunroom, leaving patients to sit on the cold floor, gazing into their navels and chanting Eastern mantras while listening to readings from *The Tibetan Book of the Dead*. Maier was known for his long hair and that he'd often roam the ward barefoot.

Government officials nevertheless continued their enthusiastic support for Oak Ridge and the international prestige the institution brought to the Canadian mental health industry—given Barker's and Boyd's stellar reputations within the psychiatric community—but behind the public facade, Barker's STU/DDT program was, by 1973, already falling apart. By 1978, internal power struggles, low patient morale, and Maier's bizarre ideas (including a mass psychedelic trip in one of the wards) and dismissive attitude toward hospital staff and security personnel led to a lockout: Oak Ridge security guards allowed no one in or out of the entire facility. The Ontario government moved to cover up the scandal, and while the STU/DDT program lingered on awhile longer with a new therapeutic format, the program was in its death throes. Maier and his professional staff were transferred out. Oak Ridge medical staff thereafter reverted to using the electroshock therapy and heavy tranquilizer regimen that Dr Barker and Dr Boyd had, back in 1965, worked so hard to eliminate.

A study into the long-term efficacy of Barker's STU/DDT program, using data collected on Oak Ridge patients ten years after their release back into the community, showed 59 percent of the STU/DDT program participants recommitted violent offences after their release. For the "psychopaths" in the program, the recidivism rate was far higher—over 80 percent. Barker's great goal to inject empathy into the psychopathic mind produced opposite results from what was intended. According to the study, the patients only learned the skills to "appear more empathetic in order to better manipulate and control others." The statistical data from the study clearly shows psychopaths, left untreated, actually committed fewer crimes than the patients enrolled in Barker's program following their release from Oak Ridge. Barker himself had, years before the clinical study published its results, repudiated his own program:

> I think you can't treat psychopaths, we don't know how
> to treat them, and you can't fix them. It's a very serious
> illness, even though many psychiatrists deny it's an
> illness...I speak of it cynically now. At the beginning
> I was a true believer...the truest of the true. We would
> all get cured the next day, the next month, or the next
> year...perhaps the people involved had to believe that.

In 2010, over two dozen former patients who had been interned in the Social Therapy Unit at Oak Ridge between 1966 and 1983, sued Drs Barker and Maier along with the government of Ontario. In 2017, Justice Paul Perell of the Ontario Superior Court ruled that the patients were indeed subjected to "torture" by the medical staff at Oak Ridge. In his decision, Justice Perell specifically ruled that the Defence-Disrupting Therapy (DDT) and Total Encounter Capsule (TEC) programs were "gross violations of their human dignity and human rights...with plaintiffs tortured both mentally and physically" during their period of detention. Armed with this ruling, the matter returned to trial in civil court for damages in 2019, but at the time of writing, a damages or settlement amount has not been made public.

Following the dismantling of Barker's STU/DDT program at Oak Ridge in the late 1970s, a hospital staff member was asked to comment on the contradictions and bizarre revelations that defined Oak Ridge. The staff member pondered the question before answering, "Hey man, it was the sixties."

***

But what happened to Matthew Charles Lamb?

Prior to resigning his position as director of Social Therapy at Oak Ridge in 1972, Barker wrote a letter of recommendation on Lamb's behalf, and in early 1973, the Panel Review Board gave Lamb his outright release from Oak Ridge. "He was given a clean bill of health. The Panel Review Board felt Lamb was no longer dangerous. He [Lamb] had been sick and was no longer sick," Barker told an interviewer. In fact, in the years that followed, Barker would tell multiple news outlets, including the *Windsor Star* and *Detroit Free Press,* that "when Matthew Lamb left the Oak Ridge facility, he had a better mental health clearance than 'you or I.'"

Once released, Lamb moved in with Barker and his family on their farm—another unprecedented event involving Lamb—for no other inmate from Oak Ridge had been accorded such a privilege. Throughout most of 1973, Lamb helped Barker fence in his considerable property, cared for the animals, and worked as an all-around handyman. Lamb regularly babysat Barker's daughter while Barker and his wife were attending social functions or on lecture tours speaking on mental health issues. Barker paid Lamb a regular wage and, combined with money solicited from his grandmother, Lamb began buying Israeli War Bonds in a calculated effort to ingratiate himself with Israeli authorities—all part of Lamb's plan to offer his future services as a mercenary to the tiny state of Israel.

While residing with the Barkers, Lamb also acted as an ambassador for the STU/DDT program, presenting himself as a successfully rehabilitated psychopath courtesy of the experimental program at Oak Ridge—a transformed productive citizen of no threat to himself or others. Ontario Police College, located in Aylmer, Ontario, is the provincial training centre for all Ontario police officers, who must successfully complete a basic training course prior to being granted full status as police officers in their respective jurisdictions. They also conduct regular training seminars for working detectives, designed to improve their investigative skills and knowledge of various topics in law enforcement. In 1973, Dr Barry Boyd was invited as a guest speaker to discuss the Oak Ridge program to law enforcement personnel. Boyd concluded his presentation on Oak Ridge's program to cure violent psychopaths to the seasoned detectives seated in the lecture hall, then introduced onstage a recently released Oak Ridge patient "no longer afflicted" by the violent impulses that had driven him to a homicidal outburst while in a state of "legal insanity." Detective Sergeant Ken Farrow of the Windsor Police Department, attending the seminar that day, was shocked to see Matthew Lamb walking toward the podium at the front of the stage. Six years earlier, on the sweltering Sunday morning of June 26, 1966, Farrow was crouched beneath an exterior bedroom window at the York Street home of Lamb's grandmother—assisting Detective Sergeant Jim Ure in arresting Lamb for the shooting rampage and murders of Edith Chaykoski and Andrew Woloch on Ford Boulevard the previous night. Farrow stood up from his seat in the auditorium and called out:

Matt Lamb, I arrested you six years ago for shooting all those kids. I was wondering if you remember that? Lamb just looked at me with a blank expression on his face and then looked away. He never said a word to the audience during the question period, instead walking over to a chair where he sat down and never looked my way again. To my knowledge, Lamb never attended any future lectures with Boyd at Ontario Police College.

In the fall of 1973, Lamb was busy preparing for his trip to Israel, hoping to join the Israel Defense Forces (IDF) upon his arrival in Tel Aviv. At some point during his period of incarceration, Lamb was somehow able to obtain a valid Canadian passport. Barker later claimed he didn't know of Lamb's plans for a career as a mercenary, but told reporters he suspected Lamb "would do something like that." Barker didn't object, as he felt the structure and discipline of a military environment would be beneficial to Lamb.

Barker's vague denial of any foreknowledge of Lamb's plan to pursue a mercenary career appears somewhat disingenuous considering that three years earlier, in 1970, Lamb immediately told his boyhood friend Hammond about his plans. As Barker was Lamb's closest confidant throughout his years at Oak Ridge—and as Lamb later lived with Barker's family—it seems likely Lamb would have confided his plans to Barker as well. However, why Barker would give his blessing, even after the fact, to Lamb's mercenary ambitions—a young man wanting to kill people for money—given his past history as a spree killer with a lifelong obsession with weapons is a question Barker was never asked nor ever volunteered to answer.

Barker once asked Lamb if he planned on returning to Windsor following his release, but Lamb felt "there was nothing for him there." Was Lamb too ashamed to return to Windsor after committing two murders and wounding two others? Future events suggest shame had nothing to do with Lamb's reluctance to return home. Rather, returning to Windsor as a released mental patient with no prospects was an intolerable situation for Lamb.

Soon after Lamb regained his freedom, the Chaykoski family learned Lamb was no longer in custody, and once again found themselves living in terror. Mrs Edith Chaykoski, the long-suffering mother of murder victim Edith, refused to leave her home, knowing Lamb was free. Richard Chaykoski, Edith's younger brother, does not recall just who notified the family of Lamb's release from Oak Ridge, but is certain the Chaykoski family was not informed through official channels—a fact Detective Sergeant Jim Ure confirms, as Windsor Police were not notified of Lamb's release either. As far as the Windsor Police Department was concerned, Lamb was still being held in maximum-security custody at Oak Ridge.

Lamb's timing for pursuing a mercenary career could not have been better. In October 1973, on Yom Kippur, Israel's holiest holiday, Israel was attacked by the two neighbouring states Syria and Egypt—an act of revenge (and to regain territory) for Israel's 1967 preemptive war of expansion known as the Six-Day War. Free to pursue his long-held desire for battle, Lamb boarded a flight in Toronto bound for Europe and then on to the Middle East. The final chapter in the strange saga of spree killer Matthew Charles Lamb was off to an auspicious start.

CHAPTER TEN

A Decade Too Bizarre for Fiction

IN LATE AUTUMN OF 1973, MATTHEW LAMB'S EL AL jetliner touched down on the tarmac at Ben Gurion International Airport twenty kilometres south of Tel Aviv, the Israeli capital. Lamb found himself immersed in a people reeling from their near-defeat in the Yom Kippur War weeks earlier. They were saved by the massive amount of military equipment airlifted into Israel from the United States, allowing Israel to turn the tide of battle from almost certain defeat into victory. Presumably, military volunteers from allied Canada would be readily welcomed in Israel at such a time.

Shortly after arriving in Israel, Lamb wrote to Dr Barker of how he hitchhiked, then walked unescorted up to the front lines where, after talking to Israeli soldiers, he quickly became disillusioned by their defeatist attitude. Military security would have been tight at the front lines and highly unlikely to welcome inquisitive Canadian tourists chatting with Israeli soldiers—thus casting doubt on Lamb's version of events. Furthermore, Lamb had invested, over a period of at least one year, significant amounts of his money in Israeli War Bonds to increase his chances of being accepted into the Israeli Defense Forces. It was a goal he was unlikely to quickly abandon after allegedly speaking to a few disgruntled military conscripts. Lamb likely invented this cover story to hide his humiliation. He was rejected from joining the IDF by Israeli military authorities—the result of failing the standard psychological entrance exam or of an Israeli background check revealing Lamb's history as a Canadian spree killer recently released from a high-security facility for the criminally insane.

Barker told the Canadian media how Lamb had embarked on a "world tour," making his way toward Australia via South Africa when, apparently by chance, Lamb heard mercenaries were being hired by neighbouring Rhodesia, then fighting a civil war against numerous Black African nationalists seeking to overthrow the White minority–ruled government. Rhodesia was indeed actively recruiting mercenaries, preferably White recruits from Anglo-Saxon or other European nations. Lamb wrote to Barker of being hired as a mercenary in the Rhodesian Security Forces, and of his joy when accepted into a "crack" commando unit: "He wanted the responsibility and respect of a battlefield command. He wanted to do the best job he could as a soldier," Barker told the *Windsor Star.*

Lamb flourished as a mercenary, serving as a commando with the Rhodesian Light Infantry (RLI), a division of the Rhodesian Security Forces. Those men who served with Lamb from 1974 to 1976 speak highly of the frail, boyish volunteer from Windsor, Ontario, Canada. Lamb was polite and respected by his peers. When not on an active military mission "in country," Lamb generally kept to himself, reading during the intermittent, boring lulls of inactivity common to war. The one group activity Lamb reportedly did enjoy was viewing a bootleg copy of the cult classic movie *The Rocky Horror Picture Show,* singing along with his mates while returning from a night patrol—"The river was deep but I swam it, Janet [...] / The road was long but I ran it, Janet." The closest Lamb came to having a friend in Rhodesia was a fellow commando, Phil Kaye, who has written about Lamb's activities while serving in 3 Commando of the RLI.

In September 1975, after Lamb had served a year in the field, Lamb's superiors transferred him to C Squadron of the Rhodesian Special Air Service (SAS), an elite airborne unit of the Rhodesian military. Lamb was one of only two Canadians to successfully complete the SAS selection process during its existence from 1965 to 1980. Sent back into the field, Lamb was now a spy, assigned to gathering intelligence by watching footpaths and seeking information from villagers who could help ascertain the location and logistical routes of the nationalist guerrilla groups opposing the Rhodesian government. Lamb confided to his fellow SAS troopers his dissatisfaction with the SAS methods of operation, while expressing fears for his own personal safety, working "out front" in an intelligence-gathering capacity. The elite troopers of SAS claim Lamb, like many of them, "wanted to engage the opposition in battle...and the SAS just weren't doing it." Sacrificing the higher wages paid to SAS troopers, Lamb threw his career path into reverse gear by requesting, and receiving, a transfer back into his old unit where combat action was far more frequent.

Lamb preferred the adrenaline rush of combat—the risk-taking factor intrinsic to the psychopathic personality. He was enjoying life, a respected member of a military unit that fulfilled his lifelong fantasies of battle along with a steady income, free room and board, and crisp new uniforms and weapons provided free of charge by the Rhodesian government. Back when he was an Oak Ridge patient and "therapist" directing a social therapy session, Lamb once spoke of his post-offence attitude toward his victims:

> Well, really, I don't feel any guilt about people I kill. I don't know them—they mean nothing to me. It's like reading about somebody in a newspaper. I can't even

> remember what they looked like or anything…the
> frustrating thing is there doesn't seem to be anything
> you can do to make up for it. Really, what can you do?
> You can't compensate them. You can't sort of make any
> restitution. They are dead, that's it.

***

In May 1976, Lamb flew back to Canada on his first military leave. Lamb's first destination was a visit to Barker's farm outside Penetanguishene. Barker's star patient of the STU/DDT program at Oak Ridge had come to show his mentor how he had made something of himself. Lamb told Barker he did not expect to see Canada again, convinced death awaited him on the African plains of Rhodesia upon his return to combat duties.

Breaking his previous vow never to return to Windsor, Lamb returned home for the first time since his capital-murder trial in the winter of 1967. He paid a visit to his uncle Stanley Hasketh, only now proudly decked out in his full military dress uniform accented by Lamb's most prized possession, an expensive Rolex watch. While still in Windsor, Lamb was strutting down Ouellette Avenue—Windsor's main commercial thoroughfare—in the RLI's green-tartan uniform with matching beret—just as a funeral procession was leaving Anderson Funeral Home en route to the graveyard. In the casket lay the grandmother of Edith Chaykoski, the first victim felled by Lamb's first shotgun blast ten years earlier. Richard Chaykoski, Edith's younger brother, was sitting in the lead car behind the hearse when he noted the soldier waiting on the sidewalk as the funeral procession pulled out of the funeral home's driveway: "We were riding down Ouellette Avenue in a funeral procession for my grandmother when I saw him. He had the uniform and looked a little different, but I never forgot his face." Word spread quickly among the Chaykoski family of Lamb's presence, causing great consternation and further traumatizing the family—especially Mrs Edith

Chaykoski. Her worst fears of the past ten years had come true. Lamb was back on the streets of Windsor. For months afterwards, Mrs Chaykoski once again refused to leave her house. Richard Chaykoski fretted over the possibility Lamb's presence at the funeral was intentional. Could Lamb be purposely tormenting the Chaykoski family once more? No one knew, but Chaykoski notified the *Windsor Star,* which ran a column about the incident the following day. If any Windsor Police detectives read the newspaper article, they failed to tell Inspector Jim Ure of Lamb's presence in Windsor that day, for the officer who had arrested and charged Lamb with capital murder believed the spree killer was still rotting away behind the dank walls of Oak Ridge.

***

Upon his return to Rhodesia, Lamb went back to the front line, where he was promoted to lance corporal and put in charge of a "stick" (squad) of four soldiers from 12 Troop, 3 Commando on Fireforce duty on *Operation Thrasher.* They monitored Rhodesia's eastern highlands for guerrilla activity. On Sunday, November 7, 1976, Lance Corporal Lamb and his stick boarded a helicopter en route to the Hot Springs operational area in Rhodesia's southeastern border region. Above the roar of the helicopter rotors, Lamb shouted out to his friend, "They are going to get me this time, you just watch, Phil Kaye!" Like his first victim, Edith Chaykoski, who ten years earlier could not see her own reflection in her makeup mirror hours before her murder, Lamb sensed his imminent fate. Two days before his final mission, Lamb inexplicably gave his prized Rolex watch and wrist compass away to Trooper Kevin Pickard. Lamb even asked his friend Kaye to witness the event.

Lamb's stick landed and formed a sweep line along a dry riverbed, slowly making their way north to a thick, bushy area where Lamb believed the "terrorists" would be hiding. As the sun set and night shadows blurred the landscape, a hail of machine-gun fire suddenly exploded from the thick brush across the riverbed, sending Lamb and his troopers to ground. Supported by covering fire from the stick, Lamb and Trooper Tony Rok moved forward to ascertain the position and strength of the enemy. Trooper Cornelius Olivier was watching carefully when suddenly a shadowy figure darted across the riverbed near Lamb's position just ten metres in front of Olivier and the rest of the squad. Olivier instinctively fired two rounds from his FN-FAL rifle at the shadowy figure. Lamb stumbled and fell, face-first, into a bush of flame lilies—an indigenous flower with six flaming red petals—which grow wild in the bushland of rural Rhodesia. Seven guerrilla fighters fled the scene at the sound of return gunfire, straight into the guns of other nearby Rhodesian forces. All seven were killed on the spot.

With the lull in gunfire, Trooper Rok ran over to attend to the fallen Lamb. Rok turned Lamb's body over, but Lamb was dead at the scene. Two rounds from Trooper Olivier's rifle had torn open Lamb's chest before exiting his back. Although killed by friendly fire, Lamb's death was officially recorded as "killed in action" (KIA). The death of a Rhodesian trooper was big news in that small nation. No one foresaw at the time how Lamb's death would become a shot heard around the world.

***

On November 15, 1976, Lamb was given a public "hero's funeral" in Salisbury, Rhodesia. Draped in the Rhodesian flag and adorned with flowers, Lamb's casket was carried in a horse-drawn gun carriage making its way through Salisbury's commercial district en route to Warren Hills Cemetery on the capital's outskirts. An honour guard fired three volleys as Lamb's casket was carried into the crematorium by soldiers of the Rhodesian Light Infantry. Senior officers of the Rhodesian military saluted while a military band played "When the Saints Go Marching In," as Lamb's body was burned to ashes.

Shortly after the funeral, Rhodesia's largest newspaper, the *Rhodesia Herald*, ran the headline THIS MAN WAS NO HERO, citing the details of Lamb's murderous past in Canada. The newspaper was immediately attacked by members of the Rhodesian Light Infantry—soldiers who first refused to believe Lamb's past as a spree killer and mental patient—now further incensed that a "fallen hero" would be disgraced by the Rhodesian media. Ian Smith, the first and last prime minister of Rhodesia, personally contacted the editors of the *Rhodesia Herald* demanding a retraction. Under assault and heavily outnumbered by Black nationalist guerrillas determined to overthrow the government, Rhodesia needed "heroes" more than ever. Three days after Lamb's funeral, the *Rhodesia Herald* retracted the story of Lamb's past and offered an apology. The politics of Rhodesia overruled the facts. Lamb's death and sordid past would not remain buried in Rhodesia, however.

The late Barbara Frum, one-time anchor of Canada's CBC nightly television newsmagazine show, *The National*, hosted a popular CBC nightly radio news program in 1976 called *As It Happens*. Frum was preparing a broadcast extolling Lamb's heroic death fighting "communists" in Africa. Lamb was to be presented as a returning Canadian "hero" of the Cold War.

Detective Sergeant Jim Ure of the WPD was sitting at home one November day in 1976 when the telephone rang:

> Well, I was at home when a guy from Barbara Frum's show calls me out of the blue. He introduced himself as Frum's assistant on the show, which I was a big fan of because it was good. This assistant starts telling me about Lamb's death in Rhodesia. Well, my God, I told him I thought Lamb was still in prison for the criminally insane! This staff member filled me in on Lamb's mercenary career and recent death in Africa. I was shocked... so were the other detectives as no one

had ever told us Lamb had even been released from
Penetang... I didn't know Lamb had been killed in
action or that Lamb's body was being brought back
to Canada, or that he was considered a "hero."[...]
Apparently, Frum was going to do this show about
Lamb, but when I filled in her researcher on Lamb's
background here in Windsor, she must have killed the
story. Her intent was to lionize Lamb as a "big hero" on
As It Happens, but once Frum found out about Lamb's
record here in Windsor, she wanted no part of it, and
that was that!

On such small occurrences can our notions of history be
determined.

Canadian newspapers featured stories of Lamb's death
and past history as a mass murderer. The widely sold American
newsmagazine *Newsweek* did a feature article on Lamb in their
December 13, 1976, issue. Lamb's widely reported death also had
powerful political implications that came to light as a result of
the media coverage. In the Canadian House of Commons, a federal Member of Parliament publicly demanded the Canadian
prime minister explain how a criminally insane spree killer was
able to both obtain, and later renew, a valid Canadian passport
while technically still in custody at Oak Ridge. Back in Windsor,
people expressed their satisfaction Lamb was not treated as
a returning hero. Richard Chaykoski expressed how "relieved"
the Chaykoski family felt upon hearing of Lamb's death. Mrs
Chaykoski could now leave her home again, without fear, and
enjoy freedom's offerings.

Lamb's ashes were flown back to Windsor and received by
Lamb's uncle. Without being specific to the media as to Lamb's
final resting place, Hasketh had the remains buried in the cemetery next to Lamb's grandmother—perhaps the only family
member who found time and truly felt compassion for Lamb
throughout his short, tumultuous life.

In 1980, Rhodesia—since renamed Zimbabwe—became a Black majority–ruled nation-state. Three years after Lamb's death, a former Black guerrilla pondered a group photo hanging on the Wall of Honour in the RLI army barracks, featuring a smiling Lamb surrounded by his fellow fighters of 3 Commando, Rhodesian Light Infantry. In accordance with new government policy to purge Zimbabwe of its colonial past, the group photo was taken from the wall and tossed into the garbage. With that, the last vestige of Matthew Charles Lamb disappeared from our world upon which he had inflicted so much pain.

EPILOGUE

OF THE FOUR SURVIVORS OF THE ATTACK BY Matthew Charles Lamb on Ford Boulevard in the summer of 1966, only Vincent Franco and Don Mulesa maintained contact with each other. Both men, now in their seventies, promised each other not to discuss the spree killings. Yet whenever they meet, the conversation inevitably reverts back to the events on that fateful night. It has remained an albatross, a repetitive ritual of endless pondering over the details of those few moments of terror more than fifty years ago, in a fruitless effort to somehow make sense of it.

Vincent Franco today resides alone in his well-maintained home in south Windsor. He suffers from survivor's guilt. During interviews for this book, Franco often ignored the topic of discussion, preferring to reflect upon his actions that hot summer night. Franco's obsession with evaluating every aspect of his movements—particularly his running to the side door of the Suchiu home seeking assistance after Woloch was shot. No matter what rationale I provided, my efforts to disabuse Franco of the notion that fear or ignorance of weapons implies cowardice, it fell on deaf ears.

Franco speaks of the nightmares he suffered until well into his sixties. They began as pleasant dreams—he and Andy Woloch going to the Hi-Ho restaurant or playing pond hockey in the once empty fields behind their childhood homes. The images of these happy childhood memories then escalate in frequency, becoming a blur of incoherent snapshots until one image clearly emerges: the terrified expression on Andrew Woloch's face moments before being shot. Franco then awakens to find himself covered in sweat.

In 1966, there were no grief counsellors to help traumatized victims heal psychological wounds. Victims of violent crime, even police officers, were expected to just "suck it up" and move on with life.

Franco has done well despite his untreated trauma. Returning to the site of the shootings just once these past fifty years, Franco immediately noted that the side porch entrance of the Suchiu residence where he first ran for assistance no longer exists, having been removed by new owners years earlier. Saying nothing, Franco looked down at the public sidewalk where the Suchiu property converges with the neighbouring home at 1872 Ford Boulevard. After a few moments of silent contemplation, Franco walked back to his car and slowly drove away, with no intention or reason to ever return. The home and detached garage at 1864 Ford Boulevard still stands, and the young sapling in front of 1872 Ford Boulevard—where Lamb stood prior to his thwarted attack on the celebrants in the Suchiu garage—is today a towering maple. The banality of the surroundings belies the horrors that still resonate in the failing memories of survivors victimized by Matthew Charles Lamb. "But looking back on it now at my age," Franco says, "it's not easy to judge someone like Lamb, considering his background."

Don Mulesa still resides in his family home on Ford Boulevard, just two blocks north of the killing site. Mulesa has refused to discuss the night of the shootings with anyone but Franco these past fifty years. The one time I spoke with Mulesa on the telephone—after he first hung up on me—Mulesa said events of the past should remain in the past, before abruptly hanging up on me a second, and final, time. One must accept Mulesa's attitude considering the horrors he witnessed that night, as we all choose to fight our personal demons in our own ways. Nevertheless, I sensed Mulesa felt empowered in refusing to discuss the shootings, unfortunately denying the historical record his eyewitness account of the Ford tragedy, for which I bear him no ill will. It is a certainty, however, that no one, including Mulesa, emerged from that life-altering experience unscathed. Don Mulesa, like Vincent Franco, remains one of Matthew Lamb's still-suffering victims.

What transpired just days before this book went to print was a complete—yet well received—surprise. I was given a copy of a letter that Don Mulesa had received from Andrew Woloch who was admitted in Metropolitan hospital at the time. It reveals Andy to be an optimistic young man expecting a quick physical recovery and imminent return to his sports teams and engineering studies.

"You rocking or what Big 'M'?" writes Andy:

"I heard stories that you have really been looking sad lately…Sorry I can't see any of you guys but it's doctor's orders. I was really in sad shape the first few days but have been coming strong the last few days. Boy, I sure have lost a lot of weight but I guess I should be able to put it back on when I get out of here. Say hello to your mom and dad for me and say hello to all the guys for me…Why don't you drop me a few lines and let me now what's happening with the Canucks, Essex County Senior League, and how the Tigers are making out. Hope to see you soon."

He signs off: "Your friend, Andy." Two days later, Andrew Woloch was dead. Mulesa hadn't even gotten the opportunity to write him back.

In the fifty-four years since, no one, not even Mulesa's wife or fellow victim Vincent Franco, had known of the letter. That alone speaks to its emotional power, of pain and loss held close and never forgotten. I hope that Mulesa finds catharsis by allowing me access to this letter. He has honoured the memory of his friend, reminding us that Andrew Woloch was a young man with hopes, dreams, and friends left behind—more than a victim of a senseless crime.

Kenneth Chaykoski, wounded by the same shotgun blast that killed Andrew Woloch, today resides somewhere in the Greater Windsor Area. Kenneth and his wife, Charmaine, eight months pregnant with their first child at the time of Lamb's murder spree, eventually split up and I do not know where Charmaine ended up. Barbara Lane, Edith Chaykoski's elder sister, today resides in a small town just outside Windsor. Lane responded to my interview request by leaving an angry message on my answering machine. Lane's gruff voice and diction suggest a life where things seldom came easy, compounded by the murder of her beloved younger sister. Lane insists she and her brother Kenneth Chaykoski want to be left alone. I have honoured her request and wish them both God's grace.

When I found Richard Chaykoski, Edith's younger brother and my boyhood friend and neighbour in the summer of 1965, Richard was living his final days, stricken with terminal cancer, but resting comfortably in a hospice in Windsor. Robert Chaykoski, Richard's thirty-eight-year-old son, married with small children of his own, today resides in the pretty town of Essex on Windsor's outskirts. Robert agreed to relay my interview request to his father, Richard, to discuss the Lamb killing spree that took his sister's life. I also hoped to reminisce about our juvenile hijinks which made those summers a fun time for both of us. Richard's son regrettably informed me his father, only days from death, still found it too painful to discuss the killing of his sister.

I was surprised when Richard's son, Robert, told me he knew very few details of how his aunt Edith had been murdered or much about the Lamb killing spree at all. The Chaykoski family had obviously concealed the details from the current generation of family members, likely seeing little point in burdening their children with the pain that Lamb had inflicted on their generation. "That event tore your family apart," I said. Robert went silent for a long time before thoughtfully replying, "That would explain a lot of things I never previously understood." The conversation was left there. If Robert Chaykoski, my late friend's well-spoken and polite son is representative of the current generation of Chaykoskis, the family's decision was a good one.

Grace Dunlop, nineteen years old, was the last person shot by Lamb while standing in the side-door stairwell of her home as Lamb ran up her driveway in a bid to escape the carnage on the public sidewalk across the street. Grace Dunlop suffered severe injuries, reportedly losing a kidney from the single shotgun blast to her abdomen. All attempts to contact Dunlop were unsuccessful.

When I interviewed him, Inspector James (Jim) Ure, a Detective Sergeant with the Windsor Police Department when he arrested and helped prosecute Matthew Lamb, resided with his charming spouse, Lou, in their south Windsor home. Jim was then in his mid-eighties, but he and Lou still maintained an active social life and were blessed with a loving family and numerous friends. Ure's contribution in providing an inside look at Windsor Police operating procedures and police culture at the time of the Lamb killing spree was instrumental to understanding the Lamb case. Jim Ure passed away in 2019.

When I spoke with him, Justice Saul Nosanchuk and his spouse lived in the Riverside district of east Windsor. Nosanchuk was dealing with serious health issues, but his eyes still sparkled and his mind cleared when he discussed points of law, particularly his successful defence of Lamb in January 1967. Following Lamb's acquittal on two counts of capital murder, Nosanchuk continued to work pro bono through Windsor's Legal Aid program in conjunction with his private practice as a criminal attorney, until called to the bench as a magistrate in 1976—a position he held until his retirement. A humble man by nature, Nosanchuk just smiled when asked if his excellent defence of Matthew Lamb had earned him "street cred" within the legal profession, considering that the defence had led to the initiation of changes to the Canadian Criminal Code's definition of the insanity plea. No small accomplishment. Saul Nosanchuk died at age eighty-three in 2017.

Windsor Police Detective Frank Chauvin, a lifelong resident of the Riverside neighbourhood, was serving in the Riverside Police Department at the time of its merger with the Windsor Police in late 1965. The statement he took from Anne Heaton the morning after the Lamb shootings, and his subsequent report of how Lamb's shotgun and shells were carefully arranged for an ambush, were the key pieces of evidence that Prosecutor Eugene Duchesne failed to introduce at trial. Detective Frank Chauvin retired from the Windsor Police in 1984, and was later awarded the Order of Canada, our nation's highest civilian award, for opening and operating a school for orphaned girls in the impoverished Caribbean island nation of Haiti. Frank Chauvin passed away in March 2015 at the age of eighty-one. He is survived by his lovely wife, Lorraine, ten children, and numerous grandchildren.

Roger Hammond, boyhood friend of Matthew Lamb, who attended the 1964 Christmas Eve party at Lakeview Marine, the store robbed by Lamb later that same evening, provided invaluable insight into Lamb's character and willingness to act on his widely known boasts of "wanting to kill a police officer before he died." Hammond became an ambulance driver prior to joining the Royal Canadian Mounted Police where he served honourably before taking a management position in private corporate security. Hammond still lives in the Windsor area and attends biweekly breakfasts with fellow RCMP veterans residing in the Windsor region.

Inspector Ken Farrow, a detective sergeant who participated in the arrest of Matthew Lamb the day after the shootings, was ninety-six years of age when I spoke with him for this book. He lived in Amherstburg, Ontario, a small town near Windsor. Farrow's spouse, a British war bride whom Farrow brought back to Canada after the Second World War, passed away in 2015. He would follow her three years later, in 2018.

Ken Farrow may have had the strangest connection to Matthew Charles Lamb, out of all the coincidences and bizarre events in this book. During the Second World War, Farrow was recovering from a lung infection in a British hospital when he befriended fellow patient and pilot Ian Smith—the future first (and last) prime minister of the White minority–ruled nation of Rhodesia in Southeast Africa. It was Prime Minister Ian Smith who insisted on honouring Matthew Lamb with a full-dress military funeral, with a garland-covered casket atop a coach drawn by white horses down the main streets of Salisbury (now Harare), the capital city of Rhodesia, following Lamb's shooting death in 1976. Prime Minister Smith would never know his Canadian wartime friend Ken Farrow was one of the arresting officers of Matthew Charles Lamb—a notorious Canadian spree killer. It is indeed a small and strange world, but one where truth always, eventually, trumps fiction.

SELECTED BIBLIOGRAPHY

Primary Sources

PERSONAL INTERVIEWS CONDUCTED FROM 2013 TO 2019.

Chauvin, Frank. WPD Detective. Interview conducted by author, taped. Windsor, ON. May 15, 2013.

Chaykoski, Linda. Telephone interview conducted by author, taped. Windsor, ON. July 8, 2013.

Chaykoski, Robert. Telephone interview conducted by author, taped. Windsor, ON. July 8, 2013.

Cushman, Donald. WPD Detective. Interview conducted by author. Windsor, ON. August 18, 2013.

Farrow, Ken. WPD Inspector. Interview conducted by author, taped. Windsor, ON. April 15, 2013.

Franco, Vincent. Interview conducted by author, taped. Windsor, ON. May 1, 2013.

Hammond, Roger. Interview conducted by author, taped. Windsor, ON. March 15, 2015.

Lehoux, Jack and Michael. Interview conducted by author, taped. Windsor, ON. August 9, 2018.

Mulesa, Donald. Telephone interview conducted by author. Windsor, ON. June 12, 2013.

Nosanchuk, Saul. Interviews conducted by author, taped. Windsor, ON. September 30, 2013.

Proctor, Alvin. WPD Detective. Interview conducted by author, taped. Windsor, ON. August 18, 2013.

Robinet, Lilly. Telephone interview conducted by author. Windsor, ON. May 15, 2013.

Shuttleworth, Jack. WPD Chief of Police. Interview conducted by author, taped. Windsor, ON. April 25, 2015.

Sweet, Gregory. Telephone interview conducted by author. Windsor, ON. November 25, 2013.

Ure, James. WPD Inspector. Interview conducted by author, taped. Windsor, ON. April 18, 2013.

*ADDITIONAL INTERVIEW DATES

Chauvin, Frank. January 8, 2014.

Farrow, Ken. May 12, 2013; June 11, 2013.

Franco, Vincent. November 13, 2013; November 20, 2013; August 12, 2016; November 9, 2018.

Lehoux, Jack. April 2, 2019.

Nosanchuk, Saul. October 5, 2013; December 4, 2015; October 14, 2016.

Ure, James. June 14, 2013; January 14, 2014; December 2, 2018.

ADDITIONAL PRIMARY SOURCES

Budjko, Oksana. Archives of Ontario. May 21, 2013.

Books

Arntfield, Michael. *Murder City: The Untold Story of Canada's Serial Killer Capital, 1959–1984*. Victoria, BC: FriesenPress, 2015.

Berry-Dee, Christopher. *Serial Killers: Up Close and Personal; Inside the World of Torturers, Psychopaths, and Mass Murderers*. Brooklyn and Berkeley: Ulysses Press, 2007.

Bourrie, Mark. *Peter Woodcock: Canada's Youngest Serial Killer*. Toronto: RJ Parker Publishing, Inc., 2016.

Brown, Vanessa. *The Forest City Killer: A Serial Murderer, a Cold-Case Sleuth, and a Search for Justice*. Toronto: ECW Press, 2019.

Capote, Truman. *In Cold Blood*. New York: Random House, Inc., 1965.

Cleckley, Hervey. *The Mask of Sanity: Revised Edition*. New York: Mosby Medical Library, 1982.

Douglas, John. *Mindhunter: Inside the FBI's Elite Serial Crimes Unit*. New York: Pocket Star Books, 1995.

Douglas, John, and Mark Olshaker. *The Cases That Haunt Us: From Jack the Ripper to JonBenet Ramsey, the FBI's Legendary Mindhunter Sheds Light on the Mysteries That Won't Go Away*. New York: Simon & Schuster, 2000.

Gervais, C. H. *The Border Police: 125 Years of Policing in Windsor*. Waterloo, ON: Penumbra Press, 1992.

Gurwell, John K. *Mass Murder in Houston*. Houston: Cordovan Press, 1974.

Graysmith, Robert. *Zodiac: The Shocking True Story of the Hunt for the Nation's Most Elusive Serial Killer*. New York: Berkley Books, 1987.

Hanna, Sharon, and Craig Pearson. *The Windsor Star: From the Vault, Vol. II: 1950–1980*. Windsor, ON: Biblioasis, 2016.

Hazelwood, Roy, and Stephen G. Michaud. *Dark Dreams: A Legendary FBI Profiler Examines Homicide and the Criminal Mind*. New York: St. Martin's Press, 2000.

Hazelwood, Roy, with Stephen G. Michaud. *The Evil That Men Do: FBI Profiler Roy Hazelwood's Journey into the Minds of Sexual Predators*. New York: St. Martin's Press, 1999.

Jordanova, Ludmilla. *History In Practice*. New York: Oxford University Press, 2000.

Nielsen, Robert F. *Total Encounters: The Life and Times of the Mental Health Centre Penetanguishene*. Hamilton, ON: McMaster University Press, 2000.

Owen, David. *Hidden Evidence: Forty True Crimes and How Forensic Science Helped Solve Them*. London: Quintet Publishing, 2000.

Rycroft, Charles. *Critical Dictionary of Psychoanalysis*. London: Penguin Books, 1968.

Salter, Anna C. *Predators, Pedophiles, Rapists, and Other Sex Offenders: Who They Are, How They Operate, and How We Can Protect Ourselves and Our Children*. New York: Basic Books, New York, 2003.

Smith, Steve. *The Psychopath Machine: A Story of Resistance and Survival*. Victoria, BC: FriesenPress, 2016.

Walker, Nigel. *Crime and Insanity in England, Vol. One: The Historical Perspective*. Edinburgh University Press, 1968.

Journals and Articles

Bahn, Scott A. "Why Spree Killers Are Not Serial Killers." *Psychology Today*, 2014.

Barker, Elliott T. and M. H. Mason. "The Insane Criminal as Therapist." *The Canadian Journal of Corrections*, October 1968.

Barker, Elliott T., and Alan J. McLaughlin. "The Total Encounter Capsule." *The Canadian Psychiatric Association Journal*, Vol. 22, 1977.

Barker, Elliott T. "Prison, Psychopaths, and Prevention." *The Natural Child Project*, 1979.

Cole, Clarissa. "Different Monsters—Serial V. Mass V. Spree." *The Criminal Code,* May 31, 2019.

Hallin, Daniel C. "Whatever Happened to the News?" *Center for Media Literacy,* 2019.

Hughes, David, Mike Rogers, Phil Kaye, Carl Henderson, and Tony Rok. "Truth Is Sometimes Stranger Than Fiction: The True Story of Matthew Charles Lamb." *Winged Chatter,* 2002.

Montaldo, Charles. "Mass Murderers, Spree and Serial Killers." *Thought Co.,* June 23, 2019.

Valpy, Michael. "Naked in the Box." *Globe and Mail,* December 1968.

Nosanchuk, Saul. "Revisiting the Insanity Defense: The Capital Murder Trial of Matthew Charles Lamb. Part 2." *12th Annual Bernard Cohen Memorial Lectures at Faculty of Law,* Toronto, 2005.

O'Rourke, P. J. "Keeping the 60s on Life Support." *Time,* January 13, 2014.

PBP Lawyers. "Ontario Judge Finds Psychiatric Patients Were Tortured." *pbplawyers.com,* 2017.

Pilon, Marilyn. "Mental Disorder and Canadian Criminal Law." *Library of Parliament,* January 22, 2002.

Ramani, A. "Narcissist, Psychopath, Sociopath: How to Spot the Difference." *Medcircle,* June 25, 2018.

Ramsland, Katherine. "Psychopathic Analysis: The Early Days." *Psychology Today,* May 5, 2013.

Satten, Joseph, Karl Menninger, Irwin Rosen, and Martin Mayman. "Murder Without Apparent Motive: A Study in Personality Disorganization." *The American Journal of Psychiatry,* July 1960.

Smith, Steve, and Alex Constantine. "Bleak House: A Case of Nazi-Style Experimental Psychiatry in Canada." *Constantine Report,* May 12, 2008.

Thrasybule, Linda. "Why Mass Killers Are Not Necessarily Psychopaths." *Live Science,* August 13, 2012.

Newspaper Articles

Bourrie, Mark. "The Serial Killer They Couldn't Cure Dies Behind Bars." *Toronto Star,* March 9, 2010.

Brean, Joseph. "With Canada's Murder Rate the Lowest Since 1966, Are We Simply Becoming More Civilized Again?" *National Post,* 2014.

Bruner, Arnold. "Killed Two in Ontario, Canadian Slain in Rhodesia." *Globe and Mail,* November 10, 1976.

Caunce, Ken, and Dick Spicer. "Charge Youth Ambush Slayer: Girl, 20, Dies: Trio Wounded." *Windsor Star,* June 27, 1966.

"Gunman runs amok—Windsor girl dies." *Toronto Daily Star,* June 27, 1966.

"Who Was the Boston Strangler?" *Huffington Post,* December 6, 2017.

"Jury told of sobbed confession." *Toronto Daily Star,* January 18, 1967.

McNulty, Jim. "Remembering…Jail Governor John Robinson." *Windsor Star,* November 27, 1976.

Scaglione, Cecile. "Second Shotgun Victim Dies: 17 Day Battle for Life Fails." *Windsor Star,* July 12, 1966.

Sutton, Bob. "Lamb Disturbed, Says Psychiatrist." *Windsor Star,* January 18, 1967.

Sutton, Bob. "Lamb Ruled Insane by Jury." *Windsor Star,* January 21, 1967.

Sutton, Bob. "Lamb Told Story of Shootings." *Windsor Star,* January 20, 1967.

Sutton, Bob. "Portrait of Matthew C. Lamb: About a Man Going Insane." *Windsor Star,* January 25, 1967.

Sutton, Bob. "Psychiatrist Testifies at Trial." *Windsor Star,* January 19, 1967.

Wanless, Tony. "Death Comes in Rhodesia: The Bloody Life of Matthew Lamb." *Windsor Star,* November 10, 1976.

Wanless, Tony. "Flashback on a Mean Kid." *Windsor Star,* November 11, 1976.

Other Sources

"Albert DeSalvo: Who Was the Real Boston Strangler?" Biography.com, October 25, 2013.

Grey, Orrin. "Who Was the Boston Strangler?" Huffpost. com, December 6, 2017.

McPhee, Michele. "Boston Strangler Case Solved 50 years Later." ABC News, July 11, 2013.

Morton, Robert J., ed. *Serial Murder: Multi-Disciplinary Perspectives for Investigators.* (Washington, 2005): Behavioral Analysis Unit-2, National Center for the Analysis of Violent Crime; Critical Incident Response Group/Federal Bureau of Investigation.

"Remembering Oak Ridge: Digital Archive and Exhibit." Waypoint Centre For Mental Health Care. Accessed 2017.

Stone, Michael. "Charles Starkweather: Psychopathic/Cold-Blooded/Multiple-Murderer." *Most Evil—S02E06—Spree Killers*, July 20, 2018.

"Was Albert DeSalvo the Boston Strangler?" *Reelz Channel*, May 6, 2019.

Woodworth, Michael, Jeffrey Hancock, Stephen Porter, Robert Hare, Matt Logan, Mary Ellen O'Toole, Sharon Smith. "The Language of Psychopaths: New Findings and Implications for Law Enforcement." FBI Law Enforcement Bulletin, 2012.

ACKNOWLEDGMENTS

IN ADDITION TO PERSONAL OBSERVATIONS AND analysis, research materials were obtained from numerous interviews with Windsor Police Major Crimes Unit officers, lawyers, surviving victims, and witnesses directly and/or indirectly involved with this case. Media archives, journals, articles, and various books relevant to the subject matter completes the secondary source references.

I wish to acknowledge my appreciation for the retired detectives of the Windsor Police Department and to Justice Saul Nosanchuk for their personal insights, knowledge, and previously undisclosed details invaluable to writing a comprehensive historical record of this spree killer case and its incredible aftermath. I hold a special appreciation for the courage shown by survivors, family members, friends, and witnesses willing to relive painful memories in the interest of historical accuracy. You have all made a priceless contribution to this book. You know who you are. I sincerely thank you.

I would like to express my great appreciation for Sharon Hanna, my editor, Vanessa Stauffer, and all the competent staff at Biblioasis.

Lastly, to the five most important women in my life: my lovely daughters, Lauren, Heidi, Oksana, and Heather; and Laura, my wonderful wife of thirty-six years whose persistent encouragement led me to undertake this book—I love you.

A retired history teacher and veteran of the Royal Canadian Mounted Police, William Toffan lives in Windsor, Ontario, with his wife, Laura, and children Lauren, Heidi, Oksana, and Heather. *Watching the Devil Dance* is his first book.